INSPIRED BY GOD

John 10 v.28
No-one will pluck them
out of my hand.

Inspired by God

by

Annette Willis

Publisher: Stinsford Publishing, BH9 3RQ. Tel: 01202 525295

Copyright © Annette Willis 2010

Please comply with the instructions detailed below regarding reproduction of this publication (e.g. photocopying).

You are permitted to photocopy the songs (music/lyrics) contained within this book for your own personal use or for use within your church/fellowship; however, I ask that no other part of the book be reproduced.

NB. When introducing these songs to your church/fellowship, I would love for you to verbally share the stories, scriptures and revelation which inspired them as I believe this will provide enlightenment as to their full meaning. Therefore, I encourage each church/fellowship/individual who intends to use these songs, to purchase a copy of this book, so that their true and full meaning is understood.

ISBN: 978-0-9561307-2-3

Printed by Book Printing UK

For more information about me, my faith and my book please visit my website **www.inspiredbygod.co.nr**

Also available on my website is the music for my songs in printable PDF format.

Scripture quotations throughout this book are taken either from The Authorized Version (The King James Bible) or from the New International Version and are marked (KJV) or (NIV) respectively. See following acknowledgements:

Extracts from the Authorized Version of the Bible
(The King James Bible),
the rights in which are vested in the Crown,
are reproduced by permission of the Crown's Patentee,
Cambridge University Press.

Scripture quotations taken from The Holy Bible,
New International Version Anglicised
Copyright ã 1979,1984, by International Biblica, Inc.
Used by permission of Hodder & Stoughton Publishers,
a division of Hachette UK Ltd. All rights reserved.

Note from the author

In years gone by there was a practice of using capital letters for pronouns referring to God (e.g. Him, His, You, Your etc.); although this is seen in some Christian books today, it doesn't appear to be the norm. Of course, I realise this application of capital first letters for words which are not 'proper names' would not usually be grammatically correct, but is something which I choose to do myself as a mark of respect for God; and for this reason I have ensured that the same has been applied to my own narrative in the printing of this book.

To clarify: as a mark of respect to God, in all of my own narrative throughout this book, all pronouns referring to God (Father, Son and the Holy Spirit) begin with a capital letter; for the opposite reason, whenever the name of 'satan' or the 'devil' is used, capitals have not been applied. However, as required, all scripture is printed as per specific Bible translation.

Dedication

I cannot rightfully dedicate this book to anyone except to God – Father, Son and Holy Spirit – for love, help, strength, deliverance, salvation, empowering, guidance and inspiration. I could not live my life without God's presence in it and therefore this book is dedicated to God, for without Him there would be no testimony, no song, and no book.

However, I would like to give recognition and thanks to all my family and friends who, over the years and especially during difficult times, have supported me in prayer. In particular, I feel it necessary to extend my special thanks to my sisters in the Lord, Joan and Rose, who for a number of years opened their home to me each week and spent many hours ministering to me – they were guided by the Holy Spirit and grounded in God's Word. I thank God that He brought these two dear ladies across my path, along with all the other people He has placed by my side who encouraged, supported and blessed.

Contents

CHAPTER		PAGE
	Note to the reader	1
	Introduction	3
1.	All that I am	5
2.	When I am alone	9
3.	Let the peace of God	13
4.	Only the best for Jesus	17
5.	In the power of His might, battles are won!	25
6.	Chosen by God	29
7.	Holy God, yes You are a holy God	32
8.	Blessèd be the Name of the Lord God Almighty	38
9.	I can achieve all things that You've called me to do	43
10.	Jesus intercedes for me	47
11.	The place called Calvary	51
12.	Love that gave itself for me	55
13.	Walk tall my child	59
14.	When I look at Your creation	63
15.	In these last and final days before our Lord returns	66
16.	When we look around us	69
17.	When I look at my life	73
18.	Speak the Name of Jesus	77
19.	We are citizens of Heaven	83
20.	This is a day of celebration	89
21.	God is mighty, strong to save	96
22.	Reminders at Christmas time	103
23.	A promise through the ages	109
24.	We're in the presence of the King	115
25.	I hear the sound of heavy rain	119
26.	Lord Jesus, I am so amazed	125

Note to the reader

The front part of this book contains the lyrics of the songs which can be read as poems or prayers of petition, consecration or praise. Preceding each of the songs, I have shared from my heart what God has shown me in many various ways over the years. Where songs have been inspired through specific experiences in my life, by revelation given directly into my heart from God or by specific scriptures on which God has shed His light to give me a revelation of His truth, I have shared these to provide insight. Also, as I have compiled this book and looked back on situations retrospectively, I have felt it beneficial to add some further verses of scripture along with more of my own thoughts to provide clarity and understanding with regards to the meaning of the songs.

The music for the songs is printed at the back of this book.

Introduction

It was some time in the mid 1990's that in a prayer meeting, held at the church I attended, a prophecy was spoken specifically to me which I believe was from God. Although I cannot recall the exact words of the prophecy, I remember the part that said I would write songs which would be sung by many.

'All that I am' was the first song I believe God inspired me to write after that prophecy had been given. Since that first song, spiritually speaking, I have spent times on the mountain tops, but I have also been through deep valleys; however, I believe that God has used these valley experiences to reveal more of Himself to me. Sometimes revelation from God has come at the end of a difficult time, sometimes during, and sometimes it has been graciously imparted before I have needed it; these times of revelation have not only taught me about God's nature and given me strength and hope, but also have often been the source of inspiration for the songs I have written.

The words of the songs which follow in this book are a testimony of God's love, faithfulness and grace to me; for He is my ever present help in times of trouble, and He is my hope for the future. As you read the words of the songs, together with words of truth from the Bible, revelations I have received directly from God and some of the life experiences I have shared, it is my hope that God will bless you and that you will be encouraged by my testimony of God's faithfulness; but more importantly, that you will be encouraged to seek God for yourself and find He is faithful to all who call on Him.

The fulfilment of the prophecy is a work in progress.
All praise, glory and honour belong to God alone.

CHAPTER 1

All that I am

'All that I am, all that I have,
I offer unto You, my Saviour and my Lord'.

All that I am – my personality, my emotions, my beliefs, my likes and my dislikes – there are many aspects to the person, Annette Willis.... me. I share my life as most do, with family, friends and acquaintances, and as they spend time with me they might think they know me fairly well; but just how transparent is my life to others? Surely for all of us, there are some things in our lives that remain within us, hidden from the outside world – secret thoughts, concealed true feelings, undisclosed sins and failings, fears and weaknesses that we have never revealed to others. The truth is that although we may keep some things secretly in our own hearts, we can never keep them hidden from God; He knows us intimately. Whether or not we converse with God or are open and honest with Him, He knows us through and through.

This first song is one of consecration and an offering of myself to God; but when I consider the opening words of the song, I realise that what I am offering to Him, (**'all that I am'** and **'all that I have'**) is actually very flawed. I know myself inside out and am well aware of all my faults and failings, and because of this – in my eyes – my **'all'** doesn't appear to be a great gift to offer an almighty, awesome and holy God.

Within this book, I will openly share some of the weaknesses in my life that, over the years, have been problematic for me; but also, I want to show how God has made provision for these things in His Son Jesus. The wonderful truth is that even though

God knows everything about me (the bad things as well as the good), He still desires that my life, such as it is, be offered to Him; but even more wonderful, is the great exchange that takes place when I have given Him my all, for it is at that point, He pours His wonderful life into mine.

The following words from the Bible were given by God to the prophet Isaiah concerning Jesus and reveal how through His suffering, He would take on Himself all those bad and negative things in our lives:

'Surely he hath borne our griefs, and carried our sorrows: yet we did esteem him stricken, smitten of God, and afflicted. But he was wounded for our transgressions, he was bruised for our iniquities: the chastisement of our peace was upon him; and with his stripes we are healed.' (Isaiah 53:4-5 KJV)

Grief – sorrow – transgressions – iniquities – mental anguish and fear – sickness. I am sure there is not one person who could say they have never been affected by some or all of these things at some point in their life; but for me, as I have personally encountered these things, I have come to realise that the resolution is found in Jesus, because He took all these things upon Himself and suffered on my behalf. I must say though, that this realisation hasn't always come easily or instantly for me; sometimes it has taken a substantial amount of time to accept the reality of all that Jesus achieved by His death and resurrection. In the verses just quoted from the book of Isaiah, one thing in particular is mentioned that significantly affected many years of my life – PEACE – or rather, the lack of it.

Peace is a precious commodity – peace in the family, peace with friends, peace in our nation and the world, peace with ourselves and most importantly, peace with God; but when peace is lacking in any of these, or other areas, our whole lives can be turned upside down and can often lead to losing our own peace of mind. For me personally, I am very aware that peace of mind is something of great value and is to be treasured, for it is something that for many years, I struggled to obtain. There were long periods when I suffered terribly with anxiety and fear; and in those times, peace of mind seemed to be out of my reach.

This may be difficult for everyone to identify with and perhaps only those who have experienced this personally can fully understand how all-consuming these negative thoughts can be; but the way I once described how I was feeling during one of those times, might help to explain: I said that it was like being in a pit from which I felt unable to escape or even look up. In those times I would look inwards and focus on the anxious and fearful thoughts that were filling my mind, and often this would seem to overwhelm me and drive me to despair. Sadly this feeling of despair often resulted in my focus being turned away from God – the very One who would be able to help, if only I would reach out to Him.

Throughout these periods I felt weak and sometimes even felt unable to pray. It was then that I valued the loving prayer support which both my own family and church family gave to me. However, I believe that to be freed of this oppression, ultimately I had to make the choice to turn once again to God for His help.

As the prophetic words spoken by Isaiah revealed, it was **Jesus** who took our *'griefs'* and *'sorrows'* and the *'chastisement of our peace was upon **him**'*.

This is a truth which needed to be deeply embedded in my heart (and still does today), that Jesus paid the price for me by His suffering and death so that I could be relieved of the burden of fear and anxiety. Although it is not easy to let go of these things – it must be done to enable God's peace to enter into my heart and reside there.

The song, **'All that I am'**, is my prayer of surrender to God, where I take all my weaknesses, fears and anxieties and symbolically **'lay them at the cross'**, (where Jesus suffered and died) and then once I have done this, to receive His peace.

All that I am,
All that I have,
I offer unto You,
My Saviour and my Lord.
All anxieties,
I lay them at the cross.
O Lord, let me rest in You.

All that I am,
All that I have,
I offer unto You,
My Saviour and my Lord.
All my weaknesses,
I lay them at the cross.
O Lord, make me strong in You.

CHAPTER 2

When I am alone

I have often heard it said that the mind can be a 'battlefield', or 'battleground'; and I know this is true, because in the past, I have experienced times when my mind has been in a state of agitation, where fearful thoughts have raced around my head at seemingly breakneck speed. If left to run wild, the effect is felt not only mentally, but spiritually and sometimes physically too; something needs to be done – some place of sanctuary and peace is desperately needed in those times of unrest and stress.

> **'When I am alone and my thoughts begin to race,**
> **when my heart begins to feel the stress,**
> **I need that holy place'**

I once had a friend, who used to talk about her 'inner room' which she would go to at various times when she felt the need. Of course, she wasn't referring to a literal room, but my understanding was that she was referring to a place within her own heart, where she could spend time with God, communing with Him.

I was reminded of the following passage from the Bible about the Prophet Elijah, whose life was being threatened by Queen Jezebel. Previously, Elijah had proved to be strong in his faith as he trusted in God, but in this instance fear took hold of him and he ran away. He came to a point of desperation and in that moment he prayed that God would take his life and that he would die. If there was ever a time when Elijah needed to meet with God, it was at this juncture; and God didn't fail him, for God came and spoke with him:

> *'And he said, Go forth, and stand upon the mount before the LORD. And, behold, the LORD passed by, and a great and strong wind rent the mountains, and brake in pieces the rocks before the LORD; but the LORD was not in the wind: and after the wind an earthquake; but the LORD was not in the earthquake:*
> *And after the earthquake a fire; but the LORD was not in the fire: and after the fire a still small voice.'* (1 Kings 19:11-12 KJV)

Of course, the *'still small voice'* Elijah heard, was the voice of God. I mention this passage of scripture because I could liken the turmoil I had experienced in my life, to the destructive forces described here – the wind, the earthquake and fire. Each of these powerful forces can cause much havoc and destruction on the earth; and in the most extreme cases, can make a tranquil place of beauty into a place of desolation. In the same way, I feel that fear and anxiety can have a similar effect on someone's life, for if left to run wildly out of control, at their most extreme, they can turn a tranquil, calm life into one which is ravaged – being devoid of peace, calmness and joy; but there is hope, for God is always there, waiting to speak words of comfort into the sanctuary of our own hearts.

My friend had found a way to commune with God in her 'inner room' and I believe that when God inspired the words of the song **'When I am alone'**, He was impressing upon me the importance of finding a place in my heart where I could commune with Him (particularly when the pressures of life would oppress me). In that place, although I couldn't audibly hear His *'still small voice'* in the same way that Elijah did, God's gentleness and love was able to reach me.

In God's Word there is a verse which says, *'There is no fear in love; but perfect love casteth out fear...'* (1 John 4:18a KJV), and it is my belief that God is the answer to overcoming fear because He not only has love, but He **is** love – perfect love.

> *'As a father has compassion on his children, so the LORD has compassion on those who fear him; for he knows how we are formed, he remembers that we are dust.'* (Psalm 103:13-14 NIV)

For me, this verse of scripture gives a wonderful insight into the compassion and love which God graciously and faithfully bestows on His children; but although it is great to read of these things in God's Word, they need to be experienced to be fully appreciated. In those times when I struggled with fear and anxiety, I came to experience for myself, God's faithfulness as He continually helped and strengthened me, even though I was coming against this same problem time and time again.

The song, **'When I am alone'**, not only describes my feelings of stress and confusion, but also what I realised about my need of **'that holy place'**, my own 'inner room', where I could meet with God. The chorus focuses on the Saviour of my soul – Jesus, and what His sacrifice meant for me.

I believe that the theme of this song is a lesson for life. There are always going to be times when we might feel pressure and are tempted to be fearful and anxious, but in those times, our greatest need is to meet with God in that **'holy place'**, where I believe He is waiting for us.

When I am alone
And my thoughts begin to race,
When my heart begins to feel the stress,
I need that holy place;
That place where I can meet with You
And know the peace You give.
Lord, I give my burdens all to You,
You give me strength to live.

Oh Jesus, You're the Saviour of my soul.
Loving Jesus,
Shed Your blood to make me whole.
Precious Saviour,
Gave Your life to set me free.
You are living, hallelujah!
Come and live Your life in me.

When I am confused
And I don't know what to do,
I just put my trust in You, O Lord,
My friend who's ever true.
In You there is security,
I praise Your holy Name
That yesterday, today, forever,
Jesus, You're the same.

Oh Jesus, You're the Saviour of my soul.
Loving Jesus,
Shed Your blood to make me whole.
Precious Saviour,
Gave Your life to set me free.
You are living, hallelujah!
Come and live Your life in me.

CHAPTER 3

Let the peace of God

During one of the times when fear had risen in my heart and taken hold of my mind, I believe that God graciously revealed a key to finding peace. This key is found in the following passage from the Bible, which is the basis for the song, **'Let the peace of God'**:

> *'And the peace of God, which passeth all understanding, shall keep your hearts and minds through Christ Jesus.'*
> (Philippians 4:7 KJV)

There have been times in my life when, like most people, I have had to face real problems or deal with difficult situations, which in turn have caused me to become fearful; but I also realise that at many other times in my life, my fears have been irrational and not based on reality. However, I believe that the *'peace of God, which passeth all understanding'* is a peace which can transcend **all** fear (real or imagined); and whatever situations we have to face, God can put His peace within our hearts and minds. This one short verse of scripture (Philippians 4:7) contains great truth as it:

- **Promises a peace** which *'passeth all understanding'*; I believe this is not a superficial peace which can be easily lost, but rather a peace which can be sustained throughout any situation and is beyond our rational thinking. Even in those times when it might be natural for us to be fearful, I believe that God can grant peace, even though we may not understand how this is possible.

- **Gives the assurance** that this peace is attainable, for it *'shall keep your hearts and minds'* – it is a solid, 100% assurance.
- **Provides the key** to how peace is possible, and that is: *'through Christ Jesus'*.

Over the years, I found it all too easy to focus my thoughts on problems, fears and anxieties – but over time, I came to realise that my attention needed to be focused not on the problem or any other negative thought, but on Jesus; and that sentiment is echoed in the words of the song as it encourages us to **'focus on Jesus'** and to **'fix your gaze on Him for He's our glorious Prince of Peace'** (see Isaiah 9:6).

I have often heard people use the phrase, 'let go and let God' – but from experience, I would say that sometimes this is easier said than done, for there have been various points in my life when I have found it difficult to let go of concerns and entrust them to God; however I really believe that this is good advice and well worth putting into practice. I expressed a similar sentiment when I wrote the words, **'Let no problem overwhelm you, just rest within His love and care'**; but even though these words could also be considered as good advice, they were actually born out of my own experience of (sometimes overwhelming) fear, anxiety or depression. I have known the sense of trepidation as I have recognised these things starting to take hold of my mind, but I have also known to a certain degree, the physical feelings that can be a by-product of fear, anxiety or depression (such as the natural feeling that someone might have when they are dreading something, like taking an exam or going to the dentist). I can still recall the dread feeling in the pit of my stomach when waking up in the mornings, remembering that all was not right; and even though I could sometimes find a degree of relief when I did something I enjoyed, it wasn't long before that sense of unease or unrest (that feeling of dread), would encroach on me until once more, I was fully in it's grip.

To be able to **'rest'** within the **'love and care'** of God may have seemed many times to be out of my reach, but the truth is that it was always available – always there if I could only relinquish the burden I was carrying and give it to God. I am without doubt that God wanted me to have rest and peace, for He sent His Son Jesus, who freely gave His life so that I might be free – truly free.

The song finishes with the positive affirmation about Jesus, that **'He is everything we need'** and **'security is found in Him alone'**; I believe this to be true, but it takes faith – faith to lay aside the things that concern us, faith to take our eyes off of the problem and faith to entrust it all to our Lord and Saviour, Jesus. In those times when tempted to despair, my advice is to look to Jesus (considering who He is and what He has done), and receive rest for your soul and peace of mind.

Let the peace of God
Which surpasses understanding,
Keep your hearts and minds
Through Jesus Christ;
So fix your gaze on Him,
For He's our glorious Prince of Peace.
Always put your trust in Him.
Focus on Jesus;
Let no earthly thing distract you.
Focus on Jesus;
He is everything you need.
Let no problem overwhelm you,
Just rest within His love and care,
Security is found in Him alone.

CHAPTER 4

Only the best for Jesus

I have found that one of the easiest places to commune with God is whilst driving alone in my car (I hasten to add, without diminishing concentration on my driving!), for when I am at home and want to spend some 'alone time' with God, I can easily become distracted. Things such as switching on the television, starting a conversation with others in the household, or making myself busy with tasks that need to be done, are just a few of the distractions that can become great hindrances when trying to set aside time for communing with God; and I believe that this is the reason why sometimes my car has become a special place where I have spent time alone with Him. There have been times when my car has been a place of prayer, where I have spoken to God concerning different needs; it has sometimes been a place of praise and thanksgiving, where I have rejoiced at what He has done; and sometimes it has been a place of worship, where I have sung along with a Christian music cassette or sung unaccompanied words straight from my heart.

It was in just one of those times, whilst driving home alone from church one Friday evening that the song, **'Only the best for Jesus, only the best for my King'**, came into being.

Jesus was once asked a question about which of the commandments was the most important; His response in the verses which follow, was of great significance and indicated something which I believe should be central in the life of every believer (affecting our attitudes, motives and in fact everything we do in our lives):

> *"'The most important one," answered Jesus, "is this: 'Hear, O Israel, the Lord our God, the Lord is one. Love the Lord your God with all your heart and with all your soul and with all your mind and with all your strength.'* (Mark 12:29-30 NIV)

My interpretation of this message spoken by Jesus is that we must love God wholeheartedly and with every fibre of our being; this is the most important commandment. Of course, our love can be shown in many various ways – by our devotion, by our words, by our deeds; and this is the essence of the song. As we recognise all that God has done for us, we should be spurred on to love Him more and to give Him **'only the best'**.

I take those words from Jesus as a great encouragement to be wholehearted in all I do for God, but there is a message which is just as clear in the following passage from the Bible, warning against not being wholehearted, or to quote the word used in the verse, being *'lukewarm'*:

> *'I know your deeds, that you are neither cold nor hot. I wish you were either one or the other! So, because you are lukewarm – neither hot nor cold – I am about to spit you out of my mouth.'* (Revelation 3:15-16 NIV)

Although there is a warning in this passage concerning being *'lukewarm'*, the song, **'Only the best for Jesus'**, expresses how my resolve to give of my best to Jesus (who is my King), comes from a heart of gratitude and is my response to what He has done for me; not only has He saved me and cleansed my heart from sin, but He has graciously upheld me during difficult times and has poured His wonderful love into my life. Therefore, my greatest response – my ultimate **'best'** is to give God the whole of my life. Of course, my best is poor in comparison to all of God's wonderful attributes, but I believe that once I've given my life to Him, He is able to graciously pour His love and power into me, by the person of the Holy Spirit **[1] *(see below)*.

It is true that we are born with natural abilities and talents, but I believe there is a time when we reach the peak of our inbuilt abilities (the things that we are able to achieve in our own strength). However, when we have come to the end of ourselves, if we surrender our abilities to God, then He can take what we have and enhance it for His glory, so that it will reach others and bless them. I feel that it would be a terrible thing to live an unfulfilled life, never quite reaching my full God ordained potential, but the good news is that God wants to empower His people and enhance their abilities (as well as giving new gifts); this is accomplished by the indwelling of His Holy Spirit – it is called the anointing **2 *(see below)* and this is what I desire for whatever talents I may have.

'...I want to give Him more – a life that's fully yielded, so that the Lord may pour His love and power in me...'
I would not want anything in my life to restrict the infilling of the Holy Spirit within me; and I know that as I give more of myself to God (relinquishing those ungodly traits and my own self will), this will make more room in my life for God's presence and power.

'...that others I may bless'
In various ways, I have received many blessings from God throughout my life, and I know that if I continue to live in Him and let Him reign in my life, I will be blessed by Him in the future; but I also realise that these blessings are not to be kept to myself – for I believe that God wants me to share what I have received with others, so that they also are blessed.

What a great encouragement it is to know that God can use this yielded vessel in His service to bless others.

'...whatever He may ask of me, may my response be YES!'

**1 The promise of the Holy Spirit (who was given to indwell the hearts of believers):

'And I will ask the Father, and he will give you another Counsellor to be with you for ever – the Spirit of truth. The world cannot accept him, because it neither sees him nor knows him. But you know him, for he lives with you and will be in you.' (John 14:16-17 NIV)

**2 The anointing. If Jesus needed the anointing of the Holy Spirit – how much more do I need the power and anointing of the Holy Spirit to do the things that God would have me do:

'How God anointed Jesus of Nazareth with the Holy Ghost and with power: who went about doing good, and healing all that were oppressed of the devil; for God was with him.' (Acts 10:38 KJV)

I feel that I must write a little more on the subject of the anointing and how, as a Christian musician, I have relied on this precious and tangible touch of God on my music. However, the principles I am about to share are not only restricted to musicians, for I believe they can be applied to all types of service done for the Lord. Every child of God (whether they be a musician or not), can take encouragement in knowing that God is able to transform any type of service done for Him.

At the age of 7, I started to have piano lessons and although nearly giving up at one point, I continued with them for about 10 years (until I left college). Around this time, I was given the opportunity to play the piano for the congregational songs in my first place of worship (which was the Salvation Army), and then a few years later when we moved to a church, I was asked to play for the worship there (which was altogether a different experience). I can honestly say that playing the piano is a joy for me, it is intrinsically part of who I am and is second nature, but more than that, it is part of my offering and worship to God.

I wrote earlier that we are born with natural abilities and talents and I believe these can be hereditary and passed on through the genes – people can be born with the same skills and talents as their parents or grandparents. Of course, our talents do have limitations, for we are all limited to what is humanly possible (even though there are some who have extraordinary skills); but there is something that can enhance the least to the greatest technical ability – and that is the anointing of the Holy Spirit. I believe that when our abilities are offered unto the Lord in His service, the Holy Spirit can enhance them so that they become something more beautiful and precious. In the case of music, I feel privileged that I had a musical training, but I am more reliant on the anointing of the Holy Spirit on the music I play for the Lord.

I remember being in a Christian meeting where a young Indian lady, after giving her testimony, was spontaneously asked to sing. She sang a beautiful, simple song and although some might say that her voice was not technically brilliant, I believe there was an anointing on her as she sang – something which made her singing beautiful as it touched the hearts of those who listened. This is what I desire for my music – not that it will be appreciated for any technical ability, but that God will anoint it, so that it will reach the hearts of those who listen.

I just want to make it clear that I am not advocating a casual attitude towards music played for the Lord (spending no time on improving technical abilities, or giving less than our best), but what I am saying is that technical ability isn't a substitute for the anointing, but rather that as we give our best to God, we need the anointing of the Holy Spirit to enhance it, so that God can speak to people's hearts through it.

I once had a picture come to mind, which I am sure was from God; I saw a person (which I believed represented me) sat at a piano, playing the notes of the keyboard. As the person played the piano, I could see there was a covering of golden coloured oil which flowed over that person continually. I realised that God was showing me something about the anointing of the Holy Spirit and how the Holy Spirit could literally envelope me with a tangible anointing. This is what I have desired in my ministry at the piano and what I humbly believe God can do as I play – not to promote any musician, but to draw people to Him.

Just to give an example of one of the effects the anointing had on me as a pianist, (something I believe God empowered me to do through His Holy Spirit) was the ability to play the piano by ear (without music). However, this was not always the case, for when I learned how to play the piano, I was taught to play by reading music and as I grew older I realised that I relied on the music as I was unable (or could play very little) by ear.

In the church I attended for 16 years until it closed in 2009, there was a great freedom in worship. Although we always had a list of songs for each service, we were open to the leading of the Holy Spirit and would sing songs and choruses which were appropriate to how the Lord was speaking to us in the service (either through the prayers of people or by the gifts of the Holy Spirit as they were ministered). The best way that I can describe these times of worship is by using the analogy of a surfer, who catches the crest of a wave, then follows it through as it twists and turns, until it reaches its conclusion. That is just how it was in those times of worship, where we followed the direction of the Holy Spirit – we weren't choosing the way that we should go, for He was in control, He was guiding the content of our worship and it was beautiful, exciting and refreshing.

As we remained open to the leading of the Holy Spirit, there were very often instances when either the Pastor or someone else would start to spontaneously sing (as they felt led), in which case, the piano had to follow their lead. I cannot remember a precise time when it happened, but I believe it was some time after coming to the church, God graciously enabled me to play the piano by ear.

Sometimes people think that if you are not born with the ability to play by ear, then you will never be able to do it – but I know that God is able to give something that wasn't there before – He is all powerful and nothing is impossible for Him; I am so grateful that He graciously gave me the ability to do this, as it was so necessary in those blessed church services, when my desire was that the flow of the Holy Spirit was not interrupted. I believe that the worship in a church should never be for the benefit of the musicians – we are there to serve God and bring glory to Him alone.

I would implore every Christian (whether a musician playing in church or doing something else for the Lord in whatever capacity), not to rely solely on natural abilities, or even abilities which have been given much time and effort to acquire and develop, but rather to rely on the enhancing, empowering qualities that are given when the Holy Spirit anoints.

Only the best for Jesus.
Only the best for my King.
Only the best will I give Him
As a daily offering;
For He's done so very much for me,
I want to give Him more...
A life that's fully yielded,
So that the Lord may pour
His love and power in me,
That others I may bless,
Whatever He may ask of me,
May my response be yes!

CHAPTER 5

In the power of His might, battles are won!

Due to the many emotional and mental struggles I have experienced (which have been like battles in the mind), I have often felt weakened in my Christian walk; however, I have come to realise that this feeling of weakness has been an unnecessary burden because Jesus has already won the battle on my behalf. What I need to do when I feel like I am in a battle and am weakened by it, is to turn my focus away from my own problems and fears and to recognise the mighty power of Jesus and consider His victory over the evil one (satan), who would try to rob me of my peace of mind.

When Jesus went to the cross of Calvary, He took on Himself everything that the devil had tried to put upon mankind; and through His death and resurrection, Jesus won the victory over sin and death. The following verse from the Bible tells of Jesus and the victory He had over the devil:

> *'Since the children have flesh and blood, he too shared in their humanity so that by his death he might destroy him who holds the power of death – that is, the devil – '*   (Hebrews 2:14 NIV)

I do believe that it is not only helpful, but is necessary for us to be aware of where our strife comes from and the identity of our enemy. I am sure that we could cause ourselves much heartache by being mistaken as to the source of our troubles; for example, we sometimes experience hurtful actions and words from people and perhaps mistakenly think that these people are our problem or our enemy; but the Bible says the following:

'Put on the whole armour of God, that ye may be able to stand against the wiles of the devil.
For we wrestle not against flesh and blood, but against principalities, against powers, against the rulers of the darkness of this world, against spiritual wickedness in high places.'
(Ephesians 6:11-12 KJV)

This verse gives us clear indication that we are not wrestling with flesh and blood – with people – ultimately our opposition comes from the evil one (satan) and all his workers. I have found that the knowledge of this doesn't make me downcast or oppressed; but just knowing where the attacks come from is in fact liberating, because I can learn to rely on God in those difficult times, knowing that Jesus has already won the battle. However, it is not enough just to know that Jesus has won the battle over satan, but I also need to let Christ Jesus have His rule and authority in my life. If I rely on my own strength and power of mind I am doomed to failure; I have experienced this many times, when my mind has been filled with fears and anxieties and I have foolishly turned away from God and into myself – I have then seemed to go on a downward spiral as I lose the battle for peace of mind. It has only been when I have allowed God back into my life that His strength has sustained me (by the power of the Holy Spirit).

There is a verse in the Bible which encourages me not to rely on my own strength, but to let the power of God – the power of the Holy Spirit – strengthen me:

'...Not by might, nor by power, but by my spirit, saith the LORD of hosts.'   (Zechariah 4:6b KJV)

The words of the song, **'In the power of His might battles are won!'** are encouraging, positive words which proclaim the victory won by Jesus and recognises the strength which God gives to me, when I live in Christ. The song also speaks of the strength which the Word of God brings whenever **'satan tries to buffet me'**; and it also talks about the hope of my future life when I will be face to face with Christ in the place that He has prepared for me.

I trust that these words will encourage everyone who reads them, not to rely on their own strength in the midst of a battle – but to look to Jesus, who is the victor!

In the power of His might battles are won!
In the power of His might I can stand!
In the power of His might I know I am strong;
When to Jesus Christ I belong.

For Jesus shed His precious blood
And won the victory!
He led captivity captive
So that I would be free.

In the power of His might battles are won...

If satan tries to buffet me
I never will despair;
For by God's Word I am upheld,
His truth is always there.

In the power of His might battles are won...

Although some battles I may face
And hard times I may see,
I know that He's prepared a place,
Prepared a place for me.

And at the end of time I'll go
To be with Christ the Lord;
Where He shall reign for evermore.
I'll worship and adore.

In the power of His might battles are won...

CHAPTER 6

Chosen by God

Sometimes people talk about the power of 'positive thinking'; well, I'm not a great believer in any power which comes from man's own positive thinking, but I do believe that God can change our thought processes so that we don't continually reflect on the negative things in our lives. In my own personal experience I found that negativity in the mind would so often open the door to fear, anxiety and depression, but I discovered that God could change this around.

Although there have been various occasions when I have gone through periods of feeling fearful and anxious, I found that as I let God have a greater rule and authority in my life, He would start to move my thoughts away from those fears and anxieties and turn them towards His plan and purpose for my future; He also gave me a greater realisation of the amazing truth that He has chosen me.

It is overwhelming to know that despite all my failings and sin, **God has chosen me** and will never give up on me. He has shown great mercy and grace towards me (something I don't deserve); and with regards to my failings – He has made a wonderful and complete provision for those in the precious blood of my wonderful Redeemer and Saviour, Jesus. He has cleansed me and given me hope that God can use even me. However, there was one particular time in my life that I felt unable to accept the truth of that; and I struggled with the thought that I had failed too many times and was undeserving of forgiveness or acceptance into God's presence.

Of course, I knew that God's Word speaks of forgiveness and how the blood of Jesus would cleanse my heart completely when I repented; but I found it difficult to forgive myself, let alone receive forgiveness from God.

It was during my struggle, that I believe God graciously intervened (which so often He has done), by bringing to mind something from within His Word to give revelation. I believe that God put the apostle Paul into my thoughts and showed me that even though he had done tremendously bad things towards the Christians, God forgave him; but more than that, God used him in His service (see Acts 22:1-21). I was so encouraged, and it helped me to know the truth, that if God could use Paul – then He could use me. Praise the Lord!

The following passage from the Bible is not only a wonderful summary of what I have written about in this chapter, but also reflects what is expressed within the song, **'Chosen by God'**.

> *'Praise be to the God and Father of our Lord Jesus Christ, who has blessed us in the heavenly realms with every spiritual blessing in Christ. For he chose us in him before the creation of the world to be holy and blameless in his sight. In love he predestined us to be adopted as his sons through Jesus Christ, in accordance with his pleasure and will – to the praise of his glorious grace, which he has freely given us in the One he loves. In him we have redemption through his blood, the forgiveness of sins, in accordance with the riches of God's grace that he lavished on us with all wisdom and understanding.'*
>
> (Ephesians 1:3-8 NIV)

Chosen by God,
I am chosen to be
His forever,
I am surrendered to Him;
For I am His child.
I am adopted as His child,
He is my Father forever,
And His love for me is…
More than I can comprehend,
Much more than I deserve,
That the Father gave His gift of love for me;
For Jesus died upon the cross
And by His precious blood,
I'm accepted within God's family.

CHAPTER 7

Holy God, yes You are a holy God

'Wash away all my iniquity and cleanse me from my sin. For I know my transgressions, and my sin is always before me...
Hide your face from my sins and blot out all my iniquity. Create in me a pure heart, O God, and renew a steadfast spirit within me...
You do not delight in sacrifice, or I would bring it; you do not take pleasure in burnt offerings. The sacrifices of God are a broken spirit; a broken and contrite heart, O God, you will not despise.' (Psalm 51: 2-3, 9-10, 16-17 NIV)

These words were written by the Psalmist, David, after he had committed a great sin; they are his honest, heartfelt and sincere supplication to God as he turns away from his sin and comes penitently back to God. I am sure that many people can identify with David as he is faced with the stark reality of the sin in his life, which is followed by a burning desire to be cleansed and forgiven; and I too can identify with him in this, because the words he wrote reflect a time when I had sinned and cut myself off from God – I had not allowed Him to have full control of my life and just like David, I needed to come penitently back to Him.

Perhaps it might seem a negative or self-destructive exercise to do as David did, and reflect upon sins committed and the heart's unclean condition; but I know from experience that it is living with unconfessed sin that is detrimental to our lives, as it creates a barrier between us and God. However, God Himself wants to help us, for the Holy Spirit shines a light into our hearts enabling us to recognise those things within us that need to be changed – He convicts us of our sin, not to condemn us, but to bring us to a place of repentance and forgiveness (see John 16:7-8). Therefore, if with honesty and sincerity we face up to our own sinfulness in the light of God's holiness and then come to Him in repentance, asking to be made clean – it has a very positive effect on our lives as we become reconciled to God.

David recognised that God did not desire from him the customary animal to be given in sacrifice, but what He actually desired was a *'broken spirit'* and *'a contrite heart'*. It was many years ago, during one particular Sunday morning service, that God used those words within Psalm 51 to speak to my sinful heart; and in that moment, my once hardened spirit became broken and I wept many tears as I surrendered my sinful nature to God and received His forgiveness. David's prayer had become my own personal prayer, and as much a reality in my life as they were in his.

The song **'Holy God'** reflects my desire to worship God in *'spirit and in truth'* (see John 4:23) and to have a heart of sincerity, whilst seeking to show my love for Him. I believe that an important part of worship is to recognise who God is and to affirm His great attributes; and in the first line of this song, one of these attributes – His holiness – is proclaimed: **'Holy God, yes you are a holy God'**, but this is followed by a very pertinent question, **'and how can I come before Your throne today?'** How can we come before a Holy God when we ourselves are not holy? Perhaps there are some who have never considered themselves as unholy or sinful – perhaps some feel that they have never done anything particularly bad; but the Bible tells us:

'But we are all as an unclean thing, and all our righteousnesses are as filthy rags...'   (Isaiah 64:6a KJV)

Once we recognise the truth about ourselves, that all our own righteousness is like *'filthy rags'*, then we should naturally become more aware of the holiness of God.

Sometimes we consider Jesus as being our friend or our brother, and this is expressed in some of the Christian songs that are sung today; but although this is true, we must never lose sight of the fact that God is a holy God (Father, Son and Holy Spirit). It would not have been possible for us to come before the Father because of our sin; and God (who is perfectly holy) could not have accepted us for the same reason – our sin; but the wonderful truth is that Jesus made a once and for all sacrifice, and through His precious blood we can receive cleansing for our sins and be reconciled to the Father.

The following verses of scripture explain how Jesus made it possible for us to enter God's holy presence:

> *'Having therefore, brethren, boldness to enter into the holiest by the blood of Jesus,*
> *By a new and living way, which he hath consecrated for us, through the veil, that is to say, his flesh;*
> *And having an high priest over the house of God;*
> *Let us draw near with a true heart in full assurance of faith, having our hearts sprinkled from an evil conscience, and our bodies washed with pure water.'* (Hebrews 10:19-22 KJV)

When we think about the holiness and perfection of God (although I wonder if we can ever fully comprehend it), it should amaze us that we who have sinned, could ever be permitted to come into His presence; it is something that we should never enter into lightly or take fore granted. It was an act of great grace when God sent Jesus into the world for us – a sinful people – knowing what He would suffer; it cost Him dearly. I feel humbled that God would do this for me – it is a truth that invokes an abundance of heartfelt worship.

At this point I would like share two images, which I believe the Lord gave me in order to provide revelation at two significant times in my life, when I needed help. I have already shared how I had struggled to accept forgiveness from God or to forgive myself of my sin; and how He graciously revealed to me the way He forgave Paul of his sin (who in his own words about being a sinner, said he was *'the worst'* 1 Timothy 1:15 NIV) and furthermore, how God used Paul greatly in His service. However, even though God had helped me in the past with this issue, there came two other occasions when I found it difficult to accept the truth of God's forgiveness and cleansing, and needed more assurance from Him. I believe that He provided answers for my doubts by putting the following pictures into my mind – I will try to describe each of them accurately so their meaning, which God revealed to me, will be fully explained:

- **The first picture** was given to me during one Sunday Service at church when we were taking Communion (Breaking of Bread/ The Lord's supper). As I put the cup (representing the blood of Jesus) to my lips and drank, I instantaneously had a picture of a person, but not as you would normally see them, for their form was like a person shown in a medical diagram, where all the veins and arteries are displayed. As I drank from the cup, I saw what represented the blood of Jesus coursing through the veins at great speed, until it reached every extremity. When it reached the fingertips and toes and the top of the head, brilliant light shone out, like rays. I knew immediately that this picture was showing me that as I received the blood of Jesus into my life, then the whole of my life would be cleansed and the light and glory and righteousness of Jesus would shine out of me.

- **The second picture** which I believe was revealed to me by God was a picture of a person (who I believe represented me), stood against a great ocean of the blood of Jesus. As I stood there facing the ocean, a huge wave (which was as tall, if not taller than me) started to roll towards me (I was seeing this picture from the side view of myself). Instead of the wave splashing against me and bouncing back into the ocean, as it would be natural for it to do, the wave went through me; and as this wave of the blood of Jesus went through me, I could see the sin and dirtiness being pushed out of the back of me. This again represented the powerful and thorough effect of the cleansing blood of Jesus.

I am so grateful to God, who graciously gave me these two pictures; they were such a great revelation concerning the effect of the precious and powerful blood of Jesus, which can cleanse the worst sinner and would cleanse me.

'The blood is efficacious' – these words came to my mind a long time ago, and at the time I didn't know what the word 'efficacious' meant, so I looked it up in a reference book. The word *efficacious* means that something is capable or has the power to produce the desired or intended result. I am certain, both by revelation (in the two images which I believe were from God) and by confirmation of God's Word, that the blood of Jesus is capable – has the power – and will produce the desired or intended result, and that it will cleanse the filthiest of hearts.

I feel the need to add one more thought at this point concerning the precious blood of Jesus: it is important to realise that having a knowledge about the cleansing blood of Jesus and a belief in its power and effectiveness, doesn't give anyone a license to sin – but the truly repentant sinner can rejoice in the fact that God has made provision for cleansing.

'...and the blood of Jesus Christ his Son cleanseth us from all sin.'
(1 John 1:7b KJV)

Holy God, yes You are a holy God;
And how can I come before Your throne today?
It's only by the precious blood of Jesus Christ;
So cleanse my heart from every sin I pray.

And now I'm free to worship You
In Spirit and in truth,
My love for You grows deeper every day.
When I think of all You've done,
And the victories You've won,
I want to bless You Lord,
And lift Your Name on high,
I want to worship Holy God.

Loving God, yes You are a loving God;
And how can I show my love for You today?
I know that You desire from me a lowly heart,
That simply trusts and wants to go Your way.

And now I'm free to worship You
In Spirit and in truth,
My love for You grows deeper every day.
When I think of all You've done,
And the love for me You've shown,
I want to bless You Lord,
And lift Your Name on high,
I want to love You, loving God.

CHAPTER 8

Blessèd be the Name of the Lord God Almighty

'Praise ye the LORD. Praise, O ye servants of the LORD, praise the name of the LORD. Blessed be the name of the LORD from this time forth and for evermore. From the rising of the sun unto the going down of the same the LORD's name is to be praised. The LORD is high above all nations, and his glory above the heavens.' (Psalm 113:1-4 KJV)

A number of years ago I was asked to lead a short session during a half day of prayer at my place of worship; I readily agreed to do this, but the very next day (almost like it was prompted by that decision), a feeling of anxiety came over me like a mist.

It is my belief that when we are planning to say something for God (to bring Him glory) and when endeavouring to build up the faith of God's people through speaking truth from His Word, more often than not, the devil will try to hinder us in some way or other. In my case, anxiety was a weakness that the devil could use to try and bring me low in spirit, so that I would back out of what I had been asked to do. However, this particular time I remained strong and despite all the thoughts which were coming into my mind, I resolved not to give up, but do what had been asked of me.

Although I started to study the subject of 'praise', I prayed that God would give me His inspiration or enlightenment on the subject, so that I could share it with the people; and I believe that one particular night, He answered my prayer. Between the time of going to bed and waking up in the morning, a short sentence came to mind as a revelation concerning praise; and as I woke, I recalled that sentence: 'Praise is like a Piñata'.

I knew what a Piñata was because I had learnt about it one time whilst working in a Sunday school class. A Piñata is a traditional Mexican object used on special occasions, and usually takes the form of a bird or an animal; it is brightly decorated, filled with goodies such as sweets and toys, and then suspended from the ceiling. The object of the game is that a child (who is blindfolded), reaches up to the Piñata with a stick and hits it until it breaks open; when it does, the children are showered with the goodies.

I had not been reminded of a Piñata since the time I had learned about it in the Sunday school class – it was such an obscure thing to have come so clearly into my mind, I believed that it must be inspiration from God. So what did the statement, 'Praise is like a Piñata' mean? Amazingly, I understood straight away what God was showing me: the meaning of 'Praise is like a Piñata' was that as we break into the resources of our hearts (our joy and our praise of God), we will find ourselves being showered with His blessings – that being, His power, His gifts, His glory (meaning being bathed in His glorious presence), and all that He wants us to have which is good.

It is not that we are to seek God for all that He has, or for His blessings – but we can't escape the truth that as we praise God, we are blessed in His presence.

> *'Praise ye the LORD: for it is good to sing praises unto our God; for it is pleasant; and praise is comely.'* (Psalm 147:1 KJV)

> *'...in thy presence is fulness of joy; at thy right hand there are pleasures for evermore.'* (Psalm 16:11b KJV)

The song, **'Blessèd be the Name of the Lord God Almighty'**, is simply a song of praise, a Psalm, an outpouring of joy from my heart because of who God is.

> '*Make a joyful noise unto the LORD, all ye lands. Serve the LORD with gladness: come before his presence with singing. Know ye that the LORD he is God: it is he that hath made us, and not we ourselves; we are his people, and the sheep of his pasture. Enter into his gates with thanksgiving, and into his courts with praise: be thankful unto him, and bless his name. For the LORD is good; his mercy is everlasting; and his truth endureth to all generations.*' (Psalm 100 KJV)

I would just like to add a final point regarding praise (one that is particularly relevant for me), that praise is an excellent antidote to fear. I believe this to be true for two reasons:

- One reason for this is that when we praise God we are turning our thoughts away from the fear which is filling our minds and instead, focusing our thoughts upon a great and mighty God, who is the answer to any problem.

- Secondly, I believe there is a spiritual principle regarding praise, for I am certain that praise is a powerful weapon against our enemy, the devil.

There is an excellent example in the Bible of praise being effective when faced by the enemy. In the 2nd book of Chronicles chapter 20, we read about Jehoshaphat, who was facing a forthcoming battle, but right at the outset, God had some words of encouragement for him:

> '*...Be not afraid nor dismayed by reason of this great multitude; for the battle is not yours, but God's.....Ye shall not need to fight in this battle: set yourselves, stand ye still, and see the salvation of the LORD with you, O Judah and Jerusalem: fear not, nor be dismayed; to morrow go out against them: for the LORD will be with you.*' (2 Chronicles 20:15b, 17 KJV)

So, God was going to fight the battle on behalf of Jehoshaphat – and Jehoshaphat had faith to believe this.

Ahead of his army, Jehoshaphat sent out singers, which he had appointed, so that they should *'...praise the beauty of holiness...'* and to say *'...Praise the LORD; for his mercy endureth forever...'* (2 Chronicles 20:21 KJV); and the following verse tells of what happened as they started singing and praising – that God brought about the victory for them:

> *'And when they began to sing and to praise, the LORD set ambushments against the children of Ammon, Moab, and mount Seir, which were come against Judah; and they were smitten.'*
> (2 Chronicles 20:22 KJV)

I believe that there is power in praise and the reason for this is that God inhabits the praises of his people (*'But thou art holy, O thou that inhabitest the praises of Israel.'* Psalm 22:3 KJV); in other words, when we praise God, God is present. God is over all and the devil has no power against Him, for He is Almighty.

There is a lesson to be learned from Jehoshaphat's actions – he had taken the Word from God not to be fearful or afraid and had faced the enemy with an army which was headed up with praise – praise to the almighty and merciful God. Therefore, when I am faced with difficult situations or problems, rather than succumbing to fear and allowing it to fill my mind, I must learn to face each difficulty or problem with an attitude of praise – but to do this, faith is required, for I need to trust that God is mightier than any problem I face.

When tempted to focus my attention on the fear which invades my mind like an enemy, I must declare that God is my strength – my focus is on Him – I trust in His great Name and give Him praise. May my life be filled with praises to the almighty and merciful God. Praise the Lord!

Blessèd be the Name of the Lord God Almighty.
Blessèd be the Name of Him who reigns on high.
Blessèd be the Name, exalted in the heavenlies.
Blessèd be the Name of Jesus Christ.
For He is high and lifted up,
His Name above all other names;
And at His Name all knees shall bow,
When He comes again.
And Lord we honour You today
And all that is within me cries:
"You are the Lord of all
And worthy of all praise."

CHAPTER 9

I can achieve all things that You've called me to do

'I can do all things through Christ which strengtheneth me.'
(Philippians 4:13 KJV)

As I look back to those long periods of time when I was deeply immersed in fear and anxiety, when facing each new day was a burden, rather than a joy – I realise that I would have loved for my life to be changed instantly; but the truth is, it doesn't always happen that way. Don't get me wrong, I am certain that God is able to do all things – He has the power to transform a person's life in an instant (whether it is being released from oppression, having the strength to give up bad habits, turning away from un-Christlike actions or attitudes, or receiving divine help for some other problem); but there might be times when we ourselves are the hindrance. Maybe inwardly, we are reluctant to completely surrender the negative things in our lives to God, perhaps they have become habitual for us, or perhaps there is some other underlying issue in our life that prevents an immediate change within us. The important thing is that we should not get discouraged when we fail, but remain open to God, allowing Him to help and give us the strength and power to change – whether it happens instantly or is a process.

The song, **'I can achieve all things that You've called me to do'**, reflects a process that God was leading me through; for He was continuing to turn my focus away from the negative things in my life, toward His purpose and plans for me. One of the main milestones in the process was the tremendous revelation I received concerning the precious blood of Jesus; that it is only by His blood that I can be cleansed and then having been cleansed, His righteousness will shine through my life (to read more about the revelation concerning the blood of Jesus, see chapter 7). I believe that the cleansing of the blood of Jesus should not be just a onetime event (at the time of salvation), for what is required is a constant covering over my life; and this is indicated in a verse from God's Word which I quoted in a previous chapter:

> '...and the blood of Jesus Christ his Son cleanseth us from all sin.'
> (1 John 1:7b KJV)

Notice in that verse, the word *'cleanseth'*; this is not past tense, indicating a previous or once only cleansing, but present tense. There is not one person (including me) who can say they never fail or have ever fallen back into sin, in one form or another. There has only ever been one perfect man and His Name was Jesus.

I realise that once I've received that initial cleansing and forgiveness of sins from the Lord (at the time of salvation), I then need to live under the covering of the blood of Jesus, so that even though I am living in a world full of sin, I can live a clean and holy life. The wonderful truth that gives such hope for the future is that my life can be a cleansed vessel which is ready for the infilling and anointing of God's Holy Spirit; and by this, He enables me to do anything that He has chosen and planned for me.

> 'For we are God's workmanship, created in Christ Jesus to do good works, which God prepared in advance for us to do.'
> (Ephesians 2:10 NIV)

It is natural when thinking about our own lives, that we look to the future and try to plan ahead; but sometimes the unexpected happens and our plans are either hindered, or prevented altogether from becoming reality, which in turn may unsettle us, bring disappointment or disturb our peace. As I look to my own future and wonder what it holds, I would love to know the exact details of how things will work out – to know the end from the beginning – but the important thing is to live one day at a time, trusting God, not relying on my own plans, but rather, seeking His. I am encouraged as I consider that not only does God have everything under control, but that His timing is absolutely perfect.

At the time of writing this book, I am seeking God's will for my future, as I do not know what direction I should take; but the wonderful truth that I am holding on to is that God has an ultimate plan and purpose for my life – I firmly believe that He has prepared in advance the perfect way for me and all I need to do is to walk day by day and step by step, following His leading (by the grace that He gives).

I need to ensure that I live close to God; spending time in His presence and letting His Holy Spirit have control of my life. I trust that at the perfect time, each step will be revealed to me as I need to take it; then, whatever He asks of me, I know that He will empower me for the task, for His Holy Spirit will work within my heart to produce the required fruits and gifts and whatever else is needed (see Galatians 5:22-23 regarding the 'Fruits of the Spirit' and 1 Corinthians 12 regarding the 'Gifts of the Spirit'). My response to whatever my heavenly Father will ask of me in the future days – my positive acclamation – must be:

'I can achieve all things that You've called me to do!'

I can achieve all things
That You've called me to do,
My Father;
For I can do all things through Christ
Who strengthens me.
And I'm living under the covering
Of the powerful blood of Jesus,
By which I'm cleansed,
So I can truly be...
A vessel that's ready
For use by the Master;
I'm willing His call to obey.
And the Holy Spirit lives within
And empowers me for service;
And He leads me and directs me all the way.

CHAPTER 10

Jesus intercedes for me

Alone – but not lonely. This was a sentiment expressed by someone who to start with, was just an acquaintance to me, but as time passed by, became a special friend (she was a Christian lady in her latter years who was a joy to visit because of her lovely cheerful disposition). This dear lady had lived on her own for a number of years, but on more than one occasion she told me that although she was alone, she wasn't lonely; I am certain this was because she had a close relationship with God and felt His presence with her.

I think it is sad that sometimes it takes a crisis in a person's life before they will turn to God, for although in His mercy, He answers the desperate cry from the heart, I believe that God wants us to be aware of His presence (and accept His presence) in our lives every day – whatever situation we may find ourselves in.

Of course, there is a blessing in having the presence of a close-knit family or friends, particularly when going through times of difficulty, for in those times we rely on their sympathetic understanding, help, love and support. There have been times in my life when I have not only needed, but valued the help of both my family and dear friends. However, there is a limit as to what family or friends can do in any given situation, and I feel there are times when it is a greater comfort to be aware of God's presence, to know that He who is greater and has authority over everything in life, is there to help in any type of situation and can provide us with the care and intervention that is needed. God the

Father, God the Son and God the Holy Spirit each have input into our lives, if only we are open to receive.

The words of the song, **'Jesus intercedes for me'** came after God graciously gave me a revelation concerning the present day ministry of Jesus; it is described in the following verse of scripture:

> *'but because Jesus lives for ever, he has a permanent priesthood. Therefore he is able to save completely those who come to God through him, because he always lives to intercede for them.'*
> (Hebrews 7:24-25 NIV)

As this revelation of truth from God was confirmed within my heart, I felt such consolation and security because I suddenly had this great awareness and assurance that I am never alone in the problems I face or in the difficulties that I may be going through, because Jesus is interceding on my behalf.

Jesus showed such compassion whilst He was on the earth, healing the sick and lame and delivering those who were bound; but although Jesus is no longer physically on the earth as a visible flesh and blood person, His compassion and power is still the same today and He has a continuing ministry.

> *'For we have not an high priest which cannot be touched with the feeling of our infirmities; but was in all points tempted like as we are, yet without sin. Let us therefore come boldly unto the throne of grace, that we may obtain mercy, and find grace to help in time of need.'*
> (Hebrews 4:15-16 KJV)

In these verses of scripture, Jesus was likened to a priest – He is our high priest – but unlike the earthly priests, who had to make daily sacrifices on the altar, Jesus was the perfect, spotless Lamb of God, who made the once and for all sacrifice by laying down His own life and offering His own blood (see Hebrews 7:26-27).

Jesus knew what it was like to live as a man on earth, He knew what it was like to feel pain, as we sometimes do; He knew what it was like to be tempted as we are, but of course, not succumbing to the temptation, He remained sinless. Because of all He experienced as a human being, I believe that He is able to understand us completely and have compassion on us, and therefore intercede on our behalf with a true knowledge of our needs.

In the song, **'Jesus intercedes for me'**, there is sentence which looks like it is in the form of a question, **'Why should I fear or be dismayed when He's praying for me?'**; but actually, rather than being a question which remains unanswered, it sounds more like a statement which could be translated as, 'I shouldn't fear or be dismayed because Jesus is praying for me'.

What a comfort I have found in the revelation that the present day ministry of Jesus is to pray for my needs and to bring them before God the Father. My positive affirmation of this is given in the last few words of the song:

> **'Every night and every day**
> **He brings my needs before the Father;**
> **And by His blood, God hears and answers every plea.'**

Jesus is exalted in the highest;
And His Name, above all other names.
Yet He knows each trial we face,
He's felt our pain and known our grief
Because as man, onto the earth He came.
He ministered in love and power,
He healed the sick and lame,
He set men free from all that bound.
But now He is in Heaven again,
His heart still full of love,
The ministry of Jesus still abounds...

Jesus intercedes for me,
When I just call upon His Name;
Why should I fear or be dismayed
When He's praying for me?
Every night and every day
He brings my needs before the Father;
And by His blood, God hears
And answers every plea.

CHAPTER 11

The place called Calvary

In many aspects of life there is the possibility that we may become conditioned to a certain way of thinking – maybe because of family opinions, perhaps by world views or possibly through customs or traditions; but I believe where the Christian faith is concerned, it is important to be open to God's enlightenment as He reveals the truth of His Word, rather than holding onto preconceived human ideas, concepts or traditions.

I have found that God has helped me greatly by making specific portions of scripture come alive to me; for His Holy Spirit has poured light upon the Word of God and made it personal to me and applicable to my situation. I have gained spiritual strength from the Word as it has been made more meaningful to me.

Some stories from the Bible are very familiar to us because we have heard them many times before, but we should be careful that we listen to what God is saying to our hearts and that we don't fail to hear what God really wants to teach us. If we allow God to permeate our thinking, then He (by the Holy Spirit) will shed light on the truth contained in scripture and give us understanding and fresh insight.

One of the events recorded in the Bible, which is possibly the most familiar to every Christian, is the crucifixion of Jesus (not only the day of His crucifixion, but also the days preceding and following it); but I believe that God can enlighten and give a greater comprehension to even this story. For me personally, I believe that God has made me aware of two very different aspects, both of which are reflected within the song entitled,

'The place called Calvary'. The two (seemingly contradictory) concepts are expressed within my descriptions of Calvary, for I describe it not only as a **'terrible place'**, but also a **'wonderful place'** – yet I believe that there is profound truth to be discovered in both of these statements.

> *'And when they were come to the place, which is called Calvary, there they crucified him...'*   (Luke 23:33a KJV)

In my natural human reasoning, Calvary was **'terrible'** because of the extent of the pain and suffering that Jesus went though because of mankind's sin – because of **my sin**; and it is hard to think too deeply about this. Sometimes however, we need to take time to reflect on what it cost our Saviour, Jesus, to go to Calvary.

> *'Then did they spit in his face, and buffeted him; and others smote him with the palms of their hands,'* (Matthew 26:67 KJV)

> *'And they stripped him, and put on him a scarlet robe. And when they had platted a crown of thorns, they put it upon his head, and a reed in his right hand: and they bowed the knee before him, and mocked him, saying, Hail, King of the Jews! And they spit upon him, and took the reed, and smote him on the head. And after that they had mocked him, they took the robe off from him, and put his own raiment on him, and led him away to crucify him.'*   (Matthew 27:28-31 KJV)

Some of us have heard these accounts from scripture many times, but the danger is that we could simply skim over them, not taking in the reality of the words. Could I ask that before you continue reading, that you re-read these two portions of scripture slowly and thoughtfully, taking on board the truth and harsh reality of what it meant for Jesus – a flesh and blood person – to experience the pain, humiliation and derision.

The awesome truth – that Jesus freely chose to take this painful route (which was the Father's will) – makes me realise to a greater extent the depth of God's love for me.

THE PLACE CALLED CALVARY

Even though we may find it hard to consider how much Jesus suffered at Calvary, it is my belief that we cannot fully comprehend how **'wonderful'** a place Calvary is (for those who will receive Jesus as Saviour and Lord), until we recognise how **'terrible'** a place it was because of what it took for Jesus to endure the terrible pain and suffering.

> *'And being found in appearance as a man, he humbled himself and became obedient to death – even death on a cross!'*
> (Philippians 2:8 NIV)

It is only when the horrors of Calvary are weighed against the knowledge that this was the place of **my** salvation, then it cannot only be remembered as a **'terrible place'**, but must also be remembered as a **'wonderful place'**; and as the last line of the song says: **'And I thank you today for Calvary'**.

> *'But God demonstrates his own love for us in this: While we were still sinners, Christ died for us. Since we have now been justified by his blood, how much more shall we be saved from God's wrath through him!'* (Romans 5:8-9 NIV)

Terrible place called Calvary
Where Jesus, God's Son died for me.
What dreadful sights were seen that day
Because the price of sin He'd pay.
The crown of thorns, the cross, the nail;
These He endured because we'd failed.
His precious blood was shed for me
At that terrible place called Calvary.

Wonderful place called Calvary
Where Jesus, God's Son died for me.
What awesome love was shown that day
When Jesus chose the Father's way.
"Father, forgive them", Jesus cried
From on that cross before He died.
Such love and mercy flowed for me
At that wonderful place called Calvary.

And I thank You today for Calvary!

CHAPTER 12

Love that gave itself for me

'...and I lay down my life for the sheep... No-one takes it from me, but I lay it down of my own accord. I have authority to lay it down and authority to take it up again. This command I received from my Father.' (John 10:15b, 18 NIV)

What a marvellous thing it is to recognise and acknowledge the great truth which is revealed in these verses – the truth that Jesus **gave** His life. Of course, as we read the accounts in the Bible of how Jesus was wounded and crucified at the hands of men, it would appear that His life was in their hands, but this was not the case – His life certainly wasn't robbed from Him – Jesus gave His life freely.

At the outset of His ministry, Jesus was led into the desert and tempted by the devil. At one point, the devil urged Jesus to prove that He was God's Son by throwing Himself from the highest point of the temple, and he quoted scripture which basically said that God would send angels to protect Him (see Matthew 4:1-7); of course, Jesus would not yield to the devil by putting God to the test. Almost reminiscent of that incident, a few years later at Calvary, mocking voices in a similar fashion, urged Jesus to come down from the cross, to save Himself, to let God rescue Him (see Matthew 27:38-43). I believe the truth is that Jesus had the resources and the power to save Himself from a very painful, barbaric death, but He was on His Father's mission (*'This command I received from my Father'*), it was a mission which required Him to lay down His own life; and Jesus was determined to see it through.

In the song, **'Love that gave itself for me'**, I reflect once more on the great sacrifice that Jesus made for me, as He chose to go all the way to Calvary.

Prior to the crucifixion, Jesus knew full well what it would cost Him to complete His Father's mission; He spoke of it to His disciples as they shared their last supper together and took bread and wine (symbolising what was soon to take place). In the days that followed, how awful it must have been for those disciples, as the reality of Jesus' words unfolded before their eyes.

> 'And he took bread, and gave thanks, and brake it, and gave unto them, saying, This is my body which is given for you: this do in remembrance of me. Likewise also the cup after supper, saying, This cup is the new testament in my blood, which is shed for you. But, behold, the hand of him that betrayeth me is with me on the table. And truly the Son of man goeth, as it was determined: but woe unto that man by whom he is betrayed!'
> (Luke 22:19-22 KJV)

We should never underestimate the choice set before Jesus as He prayed in the Garden of Gethsemane; the weight of that decision, in the knowledge of all that would take place in the days ahead of Him, must have been terrible. Within the following verses of scripture we gain some insight into the struggle and anguish which Jesus experienced, both in the words that He prayed to His Father and also in the description of this heart-rending scene in the garden:

> '...Father, if thou be willing, remove this cup from me: nevertheless not my will, but thine, be done. And there appeared an angel unto him from heaven, strengthening him. And being in an agony he prayed more earnestly: and his sweat was as it were great drops of blood falling down to the ground.'
> (Luke 22:42-44 KJV)

Surely we cannot fail to be moved when we read of the mental anguish Jesus suffered at this time. I know that I have suffered in the past with mental anguish, with fears and anxieties; they may have sometimes been over trivial issues or even problems that only existed in my mind, but they were still a terrible experience for me. However, I cannot begin to imagine what it must have been like for Jesus, the Son of God, to be faced with what lay ahead of Him.

The Bible says, *'For God so loved the world, that he gave his only begotten Son, that whosoever believeth in him should not perish, but have everlasting life.'* (John 3:16 KJV) Although I recognise this wonderful truth that Jesus was given for the world, I also reflect on it from a more personal level, that His sacrifice was for **me**.

I know that my Saviour's sacrifice cost Him dearly, and this fact I cannot ignore; it requires a response from me. My response to God is written in the last line of the song:

**'And Lord I give my life to You,
Precious Saviour, faithful and true.'**

What is your response?

Gethsemane, oh Gethsemane,
Where Jesus was betrayed.
Son of God went unto that place
And to His Father prayed,
"If it's possible, take this cup from me,
Yet not My will but Yours."
He was resolved to do God's will
And to defend His cause.

Oh love that gave itself for me,
Great love shown at Gethsemane;
And Lord, I give my love to You,
Precious Saviour,
Faithful and true.

Calvary, dreadful Calvary,
The place where Jesus died.
Son of God nailed upon a cross,
Unjustly crucified.
Yet obediently He took this path;
It's hard to take it in,
Why He should choose a painful death
To take away my sin.

Oh love, that gave itself for me,
Great love was shown at Calvary;
And Lord, I give my life to You,
Precious Saviour,
Faithful and true.

CHAPTER 13

Walk tall my child

I would like to be able to say that the first time God helped me to regain peace of mind and freed me from the oppression of fear and anxiety, that was an end to it; but I am sorry to say that where God had granted me peace, the evil one (satan) wanted to rob me of it (for I believe satan's desire is to destroy God's work). Sadly, there were many occasions when again, I succumbed to fear, anxiety and depression; sometimes those things would overwhelm me and I would feel weak once again. However, Jesus knows our weaknesses and never gives up on us (even though we may get frustrated at ourselves for being knocked down by the same weaknesses again and again); Jesus wants to strengthen us so that we can stand in faith when we are tempted to either give up or submit to these things.

There was one such time when I was going through a period of anxiety and depression; although I was still attending church throughout this difficult time, my heart was weighed down and it seemed as if nothing could lift me. However, during one particular week, I remember suddenly feeling a sense of hope rising in my heart; a hope that something was going to change in me – and it did! God intervened, and within just a few days He lifted me completely out of the anxiety and depression I had been living with – it was an amazing transformation.

I was rejoicing in what God had done, however, there was one thought that started to come into my mind: after so many weeks of going to church with a downcast expression on my face (which was a reflection of what I was feeling inside), how could I go back into the church on Sunday morning, looking as if everything was now okay? I knew that God had completely lifted me out of a pit of despair, but when I had looked so unhappy for many weeks previously, what would people think if I entered the church looking so changed – so happy?

God was very gracious to me at that specific time because He provided me with something from His Word to answer my question, something that would give His perspective on the situation. I believe that in response to my thoughts, the Lord placed two words in my mind: 'walk tall'. I felt that I should look up those words in the reference part of my electronic Bible, so I did, and when I discovered the following verse of scripture I was amazed as I realised that it spoke directly into my situation – it seemed to be tailor made for me:

> 'I am the LORD your God, who brought you out of Egypt so that you would no longer be slaves to the Egyptians; I broke the bars of your yoke and enabled you to walk with heads held high.'
> (Leviticus 26:13 NIV)

I knew this answer was from God and that it was just what I needed. This verse spoke about the Israelites, who had been slaves to the Egyptians and I felt the Lord was likening my situation to what was spoken of in this verse; but in my case, the Egyptians represented the depression and anxiety I had been bound by. The wonderful news was that just as God had brought the Israelites out of Egypt and out of their slavery, He had also done this work in my life, so that I too was freed; I was a slave no more because He had broken *'the bars of'* my *'yoke'* and He was enabling me to walk with my head *'held high'*.

This was the way that I could go back to church – with a smile on my face – because the Lord had freed me from this oppression; He had done the work and therefore I could 'walk tall'. This was the inspiration for the song, **'Walk tall my child, for I have broken the chains that once bound you.'**

The song speaks of our heavenly Father's response to mankind's sin, how He sent Jesus to save us, about His victory and how we can **'walk free today'**, which is by **'His anointing'** (the anointing of the Holy Spirit) and by **'His blood'** (the powerful blood of Jesus).

I praise God – Father, Son and Holy Spirit – for the power to deliver me from oppression; only He can do this work, and this has been my experience and is my testimony.

Walk tall, my child;
For I have broken the chains that once bound you.
Walk tall, my child;
For My Spirit lives within you.

The Father looked upon this earth
And saw men bound by sin;
But He had planned a way
To reconcile mankind to Him.

Walk tall, my child...

So God sent Jesus to the earth,
His life He freely gave.
He shed His blood for each of us,
Our eternal souls to save.

Walk tall, my child...

The Son gave up His life for us
To bring us liberty.
And when He rose up from the dead,
He won the victory!

Walk tall, my child...

So if you're bound by anything,
Just know this truth and say,
"By His anointing and His blood,
I can walk free today!"

Walk tall, my child...

CHAPTER 14

When I look at Your creation

Some people are naturally confident and have a self assurance in all they do; personally, I am not like that (although I sometimes wish I was). However, I realise that what is more important than any self-reliance, is a confidence and assurance in the knowledge that the almighty and powerful creator God, is also my creator – He made me – He is my Father and I am His child! For this reason alone, I should never have any feelings of inferiority with other people, but rather, I should simply be confident because of whose child I am. It sounds like an easy concept to understand and take on board; however, for me, it wasn't so easy because of my natural shyness and lack of confidence, and I needed God to reinforce this truth within my heart. Oddly enough, it was whilst on a visit to the hairdressers that God, in His faithfulness, provided me with what I needed – a thought which He placed within my mind just at the right time.

It may sound odd to some people, but the place where I would generally feel self conscious and sometimes uneasy, was at the hairdressing salon; I felt that the people who worked there were mainly young, pretty and confident and I felt inferior to them. This wasn't a great issue or stumbling block for me, but I believe that God wanted to teach me something about my feelings of inferiority (not something which would just enable me to have greater confidence when going to the hairdressers, but something which would be a lesson for life); on this particular occasion a thought came into my mind which I am certain was from God – 'You're a child of the King'.

> 'For ye have not received the spirit of bondage again to fear; but ye have received the Spirit of adoption, whereby we cry, Abba, Father. The Spirit itself beareth witness with our spirit, that we are the children of God:' (Romans 8:15-16 KJV)

What a difference it makes to me and my outlook on life, when I am reminded that I am God's child. If at any time I am inclined to feel inferior, I know that I must go against my own natural feelings and instead, rejoice in the fact that I am a child of God – in this I can be confident.

> 'I will praise thee; for I am fearfully and wonderfully made: marvellous are thy works; and that my soul knoweth right well.' (Psalm 139:14 KJV)

Not only has God created me and has chosen me to be His child, but when I read His Word, I am assured that He wants to be involved in my life; to me, that is a wonderful truth which gives such a great feeling of security and love?

> 'When I consider thy heavens, the work of thy fingers, the moon and the stars, which thou hast ordained;
> What is man, that thou art mindful of him? and the son of man, that thou visitest him?' (Psalm 8:3-4 KJV)

The song, **'When I look at Your creation'**, considers the wonder and beauty of God's creation and the response of praise that comes from my heart when I see it; but also the fact that I am God's creation too, and contrary to any thoughts of self criticism I may have, God's Word tells me that I am *'fearfully and wonderfully made'*. This, along with the amazing truth that God has chosen me to be His child, makes my heart respond with the words I wrote in the last line of the song:

'I love You Lord with all of my heart.'

When I look at Your creation
And I see the beauty there,
I worship You,
Just worship You.
When I recognise Your handiwork
Around me, everywhere,
I worship You with all of my heart;
For I'm Your creation too.
I'm fearfully made,
And wonderfully made by You.
Yet in love You chose me to be Your child;
And I love You Lord, with all of my heart.

CHAPTER 15

In these last and final days before our Lord returns

'And when he had spoken these things, while they beheld, he was taken up; and a cloud received him out of their sight. And while they looked stedfastly toward heaven as he went up, behold, two men stood by them in white apparel;
Which also said, Ye men of Galilee, why stand ye gazing up into heaven? this same Jesus, which is taken up from you into heaven, shall so come in like manner as ye have seen him go into heaven.' (Acts 1:9-11 KJV)

I believe, as many others do, that our Lord Jesus Christ's return to earth is imminent and therefore we are living in the Last Days. In the following verses Jesus described the things that would take place on the earth prior to His return – these things would be a sign of His coming:

'For many shall come in my name, saying, I am Christ; and shall deceive many. And ye shall hear of wars and rumours of wars: see that ye be not troubled: for all these things must come to pass, but the end is not yet. For nation shall rise against nation, and kingdom against kingdom: and there shall be famines, and pestilences, and earthquakes, in divers places.'
(Matthew 24:5-7 KJV)

We only need to watch the news on the television or read a newspaper to realise that the world is getting increasingly dark with sin and wickedness; not only that, but we have witnessed the terrible effects of famine which have become a humanitarian crisis, as well as the impact that natural disasters (such as earthquakes) have had in various parts of the world. When we see all these things, we can recognise the signs which many years ago, Jesus described to His disciples.

Although some have tried, there is no-one on earth who can predict the exact time of Jesus' return; in fact neither the angels in Heaven nor even Jesus Himself knows the day or the hour when He will return, for the Bible tells us that only the Father knows this information (see Matthew 24:36). However, I believe that Jesus spoke of what was coming on the earth so we could recognise the signs of the times. We may not know the exact day or hour, but I believe that by every fulfilment of these prophetic words, there is clear indication that time is getting shorter; therefore, we must be ready for His return.

As I have already written previously in this book, there have been so many times throughout my life when I have been distracted by fear, anxiety and depression, which in turn have pulled me away from my relationship with God; but now, believing that the return of Jesus is so close, I consider that there is no longer time to waste in worrying about issues that have no eternal worth. I have to endeavour to prioritise the things I do in my life, but most importantly, I have to put God first, making my relationship with Him the number one priority – I might not always get this right, but I need to strengthen my resolve. I have to make sure that I don't allow myself to be distracted by time wasting fears or anxieties – my heart needs to be prepared for His return. If I am living as a child of God, who is saved and cleansed by the blood Jesus, then however dark and fearsome the world might become, I know that I have nothing to fear. The day of the Lord's return is something to be excited about and to be prepared for. In the song, **'In these last and final days before our Lord returns'**, I proclaim the following words:

**'O Christian rejoice! Our redemption has come.
He is taking us home. The final battle is won!'**

All I can say is: Come Lord Jesus, come!

In these last and final days
Before our Lord returns,
We must prepare our hearts
As His own bride;
For the bridegroom is returning
To make His glory known,
And with His raptured church
He will abide.

He's coming in splendour,
He's coming in glory;
And every eye shall see Him,
Every knee will bow,
And all will recognise Him
As the King of glory now.

O Christian – REJOICE!
Our redemption has come.
He is taking us home.
The final battle is won.

There's no crying there,
There's no sickness, no pain.
What a future we have –
Those who call on His Name.

CHAPTER 16

When we look around us

> *'And there shall be signs in the sun, and in the moon, and in the stars; and upon the earth distress of nations, with perplexity; the sea and the waves roaring;*
> *Men's hearts failing them for fear, and for looking after those things which are coming on the earth: for the powers of heaven shall be shaken. And then shall they see the Son of man coming in a cloud with power and great glory. And when these things begin to come to pass, then look up, and lift up your heads; for your redemption draweth nigh.'* (Luke 21:25-28 KJV)

In the summer of 2006, my pastor asked me if I would lead the church service in a few weeks time when he would be away, (this would involve leading the worship and bringing a message from God's Word). I had done this on occasions in the past and was happy to take on this responsibility again.

Prior to the time when I would have to lead the service, I was going on holiday with my parents and nephew. My nephew (who at that time was 13 years old) had recently become very interested in subject of the End Times and the Rapture of the church[**1], so during the holiday I encouraged him to help me in the forthcoming service and share some of what he had learnt about the subject; he agreed to do this.

[**1] The word 'Rapture' is not used in the Bible, but is the term commonly known for the event of the church being *'caught up together... to meet the Lord in the air'* as detailed in the following verses from the Bible:

'For the Lord himself shall descend from heaven with a shout, with the voice of the archangel, and with the trump of God: and the dead in Christ shall rise first:
Then we which are alive and remain shall be caught up together with them in the clouds, to meet the Lord in the air: and so shall we ever be with the Lord.' (1 Thessalonians 4:16-17 KJV)

I cannot recall now how it came about, but during the holiday, my nephew and I started to write a song concerning the End Days, which would link to the message we were going to give during that Sunday service. My nephew started to suggest themes, ideas and some of the words (one line in particular was: **'and you don't know what will happen when you step outside your door'**). I took his suggestions and I believe with the Lord's inspiration, I wrote the song, **'When we look around us, see the state the world is in'**.

The first verse of the song reflects upon the 'signs of the times', which are evident as we look at the condition of the world and in particular, the condition of men's and women's hearts – the apostle Paul wrote that *'...in the last days perilous times shall come. For men shall be lovers of their own selves, covetous, boasters, proud, blasphemers, disobedient to parents, unthankful, unholy,'* and he goes on to list more characteristics that would be displayed by mankind during the Last Days, but a particularly poignant one is that they shall be *'...lovers of pleasures more than lovers of God;'* (2 Timothy 3:1b-2 & 4b KJV). How sad that these things which were prophesied are now becoming evident in our nation and in the world. The first verse of the song, recognises these things, but sees them in the light of those prophetic words in the Bible which refer to the Last Days (see 2 Timothy 3:1-5 and also Matthew 24:5-7 quoted in chapter 15 of this book).

The second verse considers the two choices which face each and every one of us: **'eternal life'** or **'eternal death'** and then a very challenging question is asked: **'eternal life, or eternal death – which pathway will you take?'** These two crucial choices are described in the following verses from God's Word:

"'Enter through the narrow gate. For wide is the gate and broad is the road that leads to destruction, and many enter through it. But small is the gate and narrow the road that leads to life, and only a few find it. (Matthew 7:13-14 NIV)

There is really no competition when considering these two options in the light of God's Word; there is only one way worth taking. For me personally, although I still sometimes fail and give in when tempted to do the wrong thing, I know that my choice must be to go the way which leads to God and eternal life – the way of forgiveness and redemption. I echo the words in the song which say: **'The best way is to make the choice to follow Christ the Lord.'**

Making the choice to seek Jesus as Saviour is something which I believe brings peace – even in these days of sin and darkness in the world. It is a choice which will bring hope as we know that one day we will be with the Lord, either when our life on earth reaches its natural conclusion (in the death of our mortal body), or at the time of the Rapture, when we shall be lifted away from this earth and meet Jesus face to face. The thought of this wonderful hope, helps to put the right perspective on my life; the hope that one day, those who have received the Lord Jesus as Saviour, shall be with Him for eternity.

> **'So seek the Saviour while you may
> and turn your heart from sin,
> for He will lift His church away
> so we can be with Him.'**

When we look around us,
See the state the world is in,
We wonder why these things occur –
The evil and the sin;
But then we read within God's Word
And all becomes quite clear,
That in the Last Days we now live
And Jesus will soon appear.

*And you don't know what will happen
When you step outside your door;
For times, they will be perilous
And danger is in store.
So seek the Saviour while you may
And turn your heart from sin;
For He will lift His church away
So we can be with Him.*

There is a decision which all of us must make:
Eternal life, or eternal death –
Which pathway will you take?
The right way is a narrow way,
The wrong way, it is broad;
The best way is to make the choice
To follow Christ the Lord.

*And you don't know what will happen
When you step outside your door;
For times, they will be perilous
And danger is in store.
So seek the Saviour while you may
And turn your heart from sin,
For He will lift His church away
So we can be with Him.*

CHAPTER 17

When I look at my life

Does God speak into the hearts of men and women today?

It is my belief that God is the same yesterday, today and forever; so if He spoke into the hearts of those people we read about in the Bible, why would He not choose to do the same today? I believe God does want to communicate with us; in fact I don't only believe this to be true, but I know it is true because of instances in my life when just at the time I have needed it, God has given me revelation of a specific spiritual truth. It has been such a blessing to know that God can communicate with me in various ways (whether it be through Him shedding light on a certain verse or passage of scripture to give fresh revelation, through thoughts or inspiration which have come into my mind, through mental images, or in other ways that He is yet to use). I am not unique in this respect, for I believe that in just the same way God wanted to have fellowship with the first man (Adam) in the Garden of Eden, where everything was perfect, He wants to have fellowship with us today – and I am certain that He has spoken into the hearts of many, as they have truly sought Him.

There was one particular instance when I was in great need of reassurance regarding a certain issue that was troubling me; I was being disturbed by condemnation for sins I had committed. I know that the Lord had previously spoken to my heart about the forgiveness of sins and had given me tremendous revelation concerning the powerful and effective cleansing blood of Jesus; and that should have been enough to put my mind at rest, and yet I was troubled again. Even though I had repented for sins which I had committed, I struggled to receive forgiveness from God; but also, I would sometimes feel self condemnation as I was reminded of past sins – they seemed to reappear in the forefront of my mind and trouble me.

In one particular place in the Bible, satan is referred to as the *'accuser'* of the *'brethren'* (Revelation 12:10 KJV), and I can truly say that there have been times when I have experienced the onslaught of satan's accusations and condemnation against me.

If Jesus hadn't gone to the cross, sacrificing His life for our salvation and providing a way that we might be forgiven of our sins, we would be a people who would have no alternative but to live under condemnation, for God could not accept us in our sinful condition; but Jesus was the solution and God graciously gave Him to the world.

We no longer need to live our lives under a cloud of condemnation, for if we receive Jesus as Saviour and Lord of our lives, if we repent from our sins, receive and live under the covering of His cleansing blood, then we shall be truly free of our sins – this is what God sincerely desires for us, otherwise, why would He have given the most precious thing He had – His Son?

It has brought me great relief and assurance to know that my sins can be completely forgiven – the slate can be wiped clean, for God is faithful.

> *'If we confess our sins, he is faithful and just to forgive us our sins, and to cleanse us from all unrighteousness.'*
> (1 John 1:9 KJV)

In regard to condemnation, God's Word says:

> *'There is therefore now no condemnation to them which are in Christ Jesus, who walk not after the flesh, but after the Spirit.'*
> (Romans 8:1 KJV)

In the light of God's Word, I am so thankful to my heavenly Father for bestowing great grace upon me; He hasn't condemned me for the things I've done wrong or punished me as I deserve, but He gave His Son, Jesus, who took the punishment for me by sacrificing His life on the cross of Calvary. I have assurance in my heart that I have received salvation from God, I have been forgiven of my sins and cleansed by the precious blood of Jesus; therefore I can wholeheartedly rejoice and say:

>**'Now there's no condemnation for me,
>Since Jesus, God's Son set me free!'**

When I look at my life,
I see the mistakes I've made on the way;
And sins of the past come back into my mind.
But when I've repented,
Been cleansed by the blood,
And sought forgiveness from God;
I know that wonderful freedom can be mine.

Now there's no condemnation for me,
Since Jesus, God's Son set me free!

Since I've received salvation,
I've been set free from sin;
Not under condemnation,
But have perfect peace within.
And Jesus, my Redeemer
Would say now unto me...
"Go in peace and sin no more;
 Who the Son sets free, is FREE!"

Thank You for Your blood,
Thank You for Your mercy,
And Your grace,
And this great salvation.
I thank You Lord!

CHAPTER 18

Speak the Name of Jesus

There is power in the Name of Jesus!
There is power in the precious blood of Jesus!

'Wherefore God also hath highly exalted him, and given him a name which is above every name:
That at the name of Jesus every knee should bow, of things in heaven, and things in earth, and things under the earth;'
(Philippians 2:9-10 KJV)

'And they overcame him by the blood of the Lamb, and by the word of their testimony...' (Revelation 12:11a KJV)

NB. Just to clarify, this verse refers to the brethren (believers, servants of God) who overcame satan by the blood of the Lamb, who is of course, Jesus.

When a very close member of my family (a child) was taken ill and was later admitted to hospital, prayer became an essential lifeline; and during the period when he was feeling extremely poorly and was in so much pain, I and my family called on the Lord in prayer many times because of this great need. It was extremely difficult to see a child whom we loved dearly, in pain and naturally, we felt very anxious and concerned for him; I'm sure that anyone who has witnessed the suffering of a loved one can identify with this. Although it was sometimes a struggle for me to remain strong 100% of the time, one thing I would say, is that without the Lord to rely on – without His support, strength and hope – I don't know how I would have coped in this heart wrenching situation.

It is my belief that if we turn to God and trust Him in our desperate times, we can have great assurance in the knowledge that God not only cares about our situation, but He also has the power to undertake for us. This is the reason why so many times we called out to God in prayer on behalf of this child, who greatly needed a touch from God.

> *'God is our refuge and strength, a very present help in trouble.'*
> (Psalm 46:1 KJV)

> *'This poor man cried, and the LORD heard him, and saved him out of all his troubles.'* (Psalm 34:6 KJV)

I am so glad that over the years I had learnt from God's Word about healing and how God is not only willing, but also has the power to intervene in the lives of people who are suffering.

> *'Praise the LORD, O my soul, and forget not all his benefits – who forgives all your sins and heals all your diseases, who redeems your life from the pit and crowns you with love and compassion,'* (Psalms 103:2-4 NIV)

The New Testament tells of how Jesus came onto the earth to fulfil His Father's will (this being prophesied many years previously). One particular prophecy (given through the prophet Isaiah) was quoted many years later by the apostle Matthew, as he confirmed that it referred to Jesus:

> *'When evening came, many who were demon-possessed were brought to him, and he drove out the spirits with a word and healed all the sick. This was to fulfil what was spoken through the prophet Isaiah: "He took up our infirmities and carried our diseases."'* (Matthew 8:16-17 NIV)

Whilst our loved one was in much need of healing, he would ask time and time again for us to pray for him – which we did fervently; but apart from our own prayers, it was also very reassuring to know that we had the prayer support from other members of our family, friends and the church – this was not only needed, but greatly appreciated. I believe that it is important when there is a need, for the body of Christ (His followers) to support one another; not only by showing compassion and practical acts of love and care, but by bringing these matters to God in prayer, as He is the ultimate source of help and strength. Having been a recipient of this support, I recognise that I need to have the same consideration for others when they have a need.

Apart from our own prayers and the prayer support that we received from family and friends, we also remembered the things we had learnt previously from God's Word concerning healing; and so we put this knowledge into action, as we did everything that we knew how to do:

- We prayed for healing with the laying on of hands.
  '...they shall lay hands on the sick, and they shall recover.'
  (Mark 16:18b KJV)

- We anointed with oil.
  '...and anointed with oil many that were sick, and healed them.'
  (Mark 6:13b KJV)

- We shared the emblems of Communion together.
  '...That the Lord Jesus the same night in which he was betrayed took bread:
  And when he had given thanks, he brake it, and said, Take, eat: this is my body, which is broken for you: this do in remembrance of me. After the same manner also he took the cup, when he had supped, saying, This cup is the new testament in my blood: this do ye, as oft as ye drink it, in remembrance of me. For as often as ye eat this bread, and drink this cup, ye do shew the Lord's death till he come.'   (1 Corinthians 11:23b-26 KJV)

When Jesus shed His blood for us, this was a new covenant which not only meant that we could be forgiven of sin, but healed of our sicknesses; so in taking these emblems, we were remembering that:

'...he was wounded for our transgressions, he was bruised for our iniquities: the chastisement of our peace was upon him; and with his stripes we are healed.' (Isaiah 53:5 KJV)

- We recognised the power that there is in the Name of Jesus and also in the precious blood of Jesus; and when we prayed, we prayed in His Name and pleaded His blood **[1] over our loved one (see the Bible verses quoted at the beginning of this chapter).

**[1] The term, 'plead the blood', is one that sadly is not very often heard today, but what saddens me even more is the possibility that because this term has seemingly fallen into disuse, some Christians might be unaware of its meaning. To explain:- my understanding of what it means to 'plead the blood of Jesus' is simply to proclaim or speak out the virtues of His blood (as recorded in the Word of God) over situations where protection, healing or cleansing is needed; by doing this, we are not only speaking of, or encouraging ourselves about the virtues of the precious blood of Jesus, but by faith, we are putting the things in our lives (or in the lives of those we are praying for) under the power and authority which has been given through the blood of Jesus. It is amazing what Jesus accomplished at Calvary by the shedding of His blood and I believe that it is advantageous for us to read about the blood of Jesus in God's Word; as we do this and allow the Holy Spirit to confirm the truth within our hearts, this enables us to speak out with knowledge and assurance of the truth.

After the first week in hospital, where there appeared to be no improvement in our loved one's condition, he suddenly seemed to turn a corner and throughout the next week, day by day, he started to get better. I believe that it was through the prayers of

God's people and the faithfulness of God in confirming the truth contained within His Word, that our loved one was restored back to full health. The doctors found the right medication to treat his condition and I believe that it was God who brought about a swift and complete recovery. We rejoiced in it and gave thanks to God!

The song, **'Speak the Name of Jesus'**, was completed by the end of May 2005, which was just a short time before our loved one developed this condition, towards the end of June 2005. The words I had written, which I believe God had graciously inspired, became a living reality as we spoke the Name of Jesus, prayed the Name of Jesus, declared the Name of Jesus and pleaded and proclaimed the precious blood of Jesus over the situation.

I praise and thank God for the love and care that He pours out faithfully to His children – for His Word, from which we can receive truth and strength – and for Jesus, who became for us a sacrifice and took on Himself our sins and sicknesses. The Name of Jesus is above every name and I am glad that I can confidently proclaim His authority over the situations that arise in my life.

Speak the Name of Jesus,
Pray the Name of Jesus,
Declare the Name of Jesus;
For He is the King.
And His Name is mighty,
And above all others.
He is worthy of all praise,
He's been exalted to the highest place.
The precious Name of Jesus thrills my heart.

Plead the blood of Jesus,
Precious blood of Jesus,
Proclaim the blood of Jesus over all your life;
For His blood is cleansing,
And it is redeeming.
Our Lord shed His blood for me
When He was crucified at Calvary.
There's life and power in Jesus' precious blood.

CHAPTER 19

We are citizens of Heaven

It is good when Christian brothers and sisters can share the things of God together, for we each have different experiences in life, different examples of God's intervention in our various situations, and we can testify to the different ways that God's Word has spoken to us; these things can be instrumental in building each other up in faith. At the church I attended for a number of years, we were sometimes given the opportunity to share (as we felt led by the Holy Spirit) during an 'Open Ministry' Service; some might read a few verses from the Bible and then continue to expound upon them, some might read a Christian article or perhaps a poem and share how it had blessed them, others might give a testimony of God's intervention in their lives, or there might even be someone who would sing.

It is easy for us to sit back in the church pews each week and receive God's Word from the Pastor (or whoever might be ministering), but I feel that sometimes it is good to have the challenge of seeking God ourselves; and I personally found it very beneficial when there was going to be a time of 'open ministry' in the church, to seek God for something to share with the congregation – something that I believed He wanted to say to the church through me. On these occasions I felt that when I truly asked God for inspiration and guidance, He didn't fail me.

In November 2004 I was asked to lead an evening service in which we were having 'open ministry'; this would involve leading the congregation in a time of worship, encouraging people to share whatever the Lord had laid on their hearts and then (as was the norm), bring the service to a conclusion by sharing a message from God's Word myself. I had previously written a song about being prepared for the Second Coming of Jesus (see chapter 15 – **'In these last and final days before our Lord returns'**), and as I sought God as to what I should speak about in the forthcoming service, this subject came once again into my mind; however, I believed that I should not only consider the return of Jesus to the earth, but also reflect on the work that He wants us to do before He returns. As I was now certain of what the theme of my message should be, I began to study and meditate on it.

I said in a previous chapter that one of the easiest places I found to commune with God was whilst driving alone in my car, but another place which I found to be equally good, was out in the fresh air, walking on my own; and as I walked home from work one particular day, wanting to make good use of this valuable (if short) time slot, I began to reflect on a verse of scripture which was key to my message:

'But our citizenship is in heaven. And we eagerly await a Saviour from there, the Lord Jesus Christ,'
(Philippians 3:20 NIV)

As I was reflecting on this verse, I felt the Lord beginning to inspire me with a new song; it started to fill my mind and actually evolved very quickly. By the day of the Open Ministry Service, I had completed the song – it started with the following words: **'We are citizens of Heaven and our Lord is coming soon'**. I was so pleased that it had been completed in time because I would be able to emphasize the point of the message with a song which I believe the Lord had inspired.

Prior to the time when I was preparing the message from God's Word, I had felt that pressure and stress had been crowding in on me, as anxieties and concerns about my job filled my mind; in fact, I had found it hard to concentrate on anything else. However, it was good to begin focussing on something which I believed was from God, for I am certain that He was directing my thoughts and leading me into what I should share with the church; having said that, I do not believe that this message was for them alone, for I realise that it was also for my own spiritual growth and strengthening. God wanted to emphasize to me where my attention should really be.

I started to understand how pointless it was to be consumed with worry about work and other such things that had no eternal worth; instead, my mind needed to be focussed on the things of God – the things which had eternal value in His eyes.

It can be all too easy to become preoccupied with worries and concerns about our earthly lives and sometimes we can lose sight of what is really important from God's perspective. Of course, we have day to day responsibilities and tasks, which we should carry out as if unto God (see Colossians 3:23), but our priority in life should not be for those earthly things; it should be for the things of God's kingdom, which will matter for eternity.

You only have to read the newspapers or watch the news to recognize the fact that there are many people in the world today who are living for the moment and not taking any thought about tomorrow; sometimes they try extreme ways to seek pleasure and fulfilment, such as drugs or alcohol. The following verse from God's Word, although written many years ago, seems to reflect the things which are happening today in our generation:

> *'For, as I have often told you before and now say again even with tears, many live as enemies of the cross of Christ. Their destiny is destruction, their god is their stomach, and their glory is in their shame. Their mind is on earthly things. But our citizenship is in heaven. And we eagerly await a Saviour from there, the Lord Jesus Christ,'* (Philippians 3:18-20 NIV)

I am so grateful to God (and it is only by His grace) that I have been kept from going down the route of taking drugs or alcohol in a vain bid to find relief from the troubles I have experienced, for I realise they cannot bring lasting satisfaction, fulfilment or peace; I believe these things are from God and can only enter our lives as we accept Jesus, not only as our Saviour, but also as our Lord (which means allowing God to have authority over our lives). The effect of this is that God not only brings peace into our hearts, but also gives us the assurance of an eternal hope that is found in Jesus.

We live in a beautiful world that God created and which we enjoy, but we must realise this is only our temporary accommodation; we have an eternal home, which is Heaven. The apostle Paul once wrote the following words concerning this matter:

> *'Set your affection on things above, not on things on the earth. For ye are dead, and your life is hid with Christ in God. When Christ, who is our life, shall appear, then shall ye also appear with him in glory.'* (Colossians 3:2-4 KJV)

I believe those words can bring comfort to anyone who suffers with anxiety or fear (as I have done in past years), as they help us to view things in their correct perspective; earthly things are passing, but our life in Jesus will last for eternity – this should be our number one priority and our joy. However, there is another step which we, as children of God, should take and (as I have indicated earlier in this book), is something which I have personally found very helpful in combating the negative things in my mind; that is to consider the positive things which are found in God's plans and purposes and then, work to achieve them with God's help.

When Jesus came to earth, even He was seeking to fulfil the plans and purposes His Father had for Him – He was on a mission. In just 33 years on the earth, from His birth to His death (and only a few of those years actually in ministry), Jesus would not only provide an example for mankind to live by, but would fulfil the Father's plan to purchase our salvation by His death and resurrection. However, Jesus knew that when He returned to His Father, His disciples, who had been with Him throughout His ministry, would be left on the earth; and in the book of John in God's Word, we read a heartfelt prayer which Jesus prayed, as His mission was coming to its conclusion – He prayed for His disciples and indicated the plan and purpose God had for their lives in the future:

> *'They are not of the world, even as I am not of the world. Sanctify them through thy truth: thy word is truth. As thou hast sent me into the world, even so have I also sent them into the world.'* (John17:16-18 KJV)

According to His Father's will, Jesus accomplished His part of the mission on earth, but the Father's plan did not end there, for the disciples of Jesus had been specially chosen to continue a work on the earth. Just before Jesus was taken up into Heaven, He appeared to His disciples and gave them instruction for the mission that lay ahead of them – the 'great commission' as it is often referred to (see Mark 16:15-18). The disciples proved their faithfulness in the work God had planned for them, but the mission didn't stop with them, for I believe that until the Lord returns, there is still work to be done; as I wrote in the song, **'He gave the great commission which still is ours today and the Holy Spirit gives us power to serve in every way'**.

My priority in life must be to seek God's will – to make the important decision to serve Him – and with the Holy Spirit's empowerment, work to fulfil the plans He has for my life, with devotion and passion.

We are citizens of Heaven
And our Lord is coming soon.
He will lift us up from all the earth
And take our fear and gloom.
It will be such joy to see Him,
But remember this, my friend,
Before the Lord returns,
There's work to do;
For He gave the great commission,
Which still we must obey,
And the Holy Spirit gives us power
To serve in every way.
So choose to do His perfect will
And know this truth today...
We are citizens of Heaven
And not of earth.

CHAPTER 20

This is a day of celebration

'Procrastination is the thief of time!'

I never met my great-grandfather, but I am told that this was one of the sayings he often used. Of course now-a-days, some of these sayings might be considered as being old-fashioned, but far from being outdated, I think this particular saying still has great truth in it; for I guess there have been times when most, if not all of us, have put off until tomorrow those things we should do today (of course, sometimes it bears little importance that we have done this, but on other occasions, it is possible that our procrastination could have a detrimental effect). I experienced this for myself at one particular time when there was some issue I hadn't dealt with – it was a difficult situation I had been putting off for quite a while. As time went by, I tried to put this unresolved issue to the back of my mind; but the effect this had on me was that I couldn't enjoy complete peace – it was always there in my mind (not always to the forefront, because there were times when I managed to put the matter right to the back of my mind, but sometimes it would fill my thoughts and cause great distress). Yes, I can easily identify with the saying 'Procrastination is the thief of time', because as I look back on the situation now, it seems as if precious moments of time (in which I could have had peace of mind) had been stolen from me because I had put off dealing with the matter. However, the day came when, even though I was dreading having to face this difficult situation, I knew that I must; once and for all, it had to be dealt with so that it could have no further hold on me.

It is comforting to know that God is aware of every situation we face and has compassion on us, His children; I believe that He knew the stress I was experiencing and sent consolation to my heart as He inspired the words of the song **'This is a day of celebration'**. The message within the song is clear – God was showing me that whatever situation I might find myself in (good or bad), or whatever problem I might have to face, I should look to the good things that He has done for me; I should remind myself of how much God has given and then thank Him and praise Him.

> *'...Sing and make music in your heart to the Lord, always giving thanks to God the Father for everything, in the name of our Lord Jesus Christ.'* (Ephesians 5:19b-20 NIV)

The words in the first verse of the song say:
'I won't worry about the past...'
There have been many times in my life when I have let concerns of the past spoil my today. I realise now that this is such an unproductive practice, as nothing good comes from it; most of the time there is nothing we can do to change the problems of the past and dwelling on them can severely limit our capacity for experiencing peace of mind and joy in the present. However, there is a very encouraging passage of scripture which God impressed upon my heart one other time, when I was concerned about things that had happened previously; it was a time when I needed to let go of cares and worries about the past and look to the future which God had already planned:

> *'...but this one thing I do, forgetting those things which are behind, and reaching forth unto those things which are before, I press toward the mark for the prize of the high calling of God in Christ Jesus.'* (Philippians 3:13b-14 KJV)

There is a tremendous reassurance in knowing that once we give our lives to God and 'live in Christ', then although we may have to deal with issues from the past (and if required, do whatever it takes to put things right), these things can no longer have any hold over us – there is no-one who can justly condemn us – for God has made us new:

> *'Therefore if any man be in Christ, he is a new creature: old things are passed away; behold, all things are become new.'*
> (2 Corinthians 5:17 KJV)

Going back to the song, the second verse says:
'I won't worry about the future…'
Just as it is pointless to worry about the past, so it is to worry about the future. I have experienced both and can say that they are both equally pointless, but also destructive. Jesus Himself gave some good succinct advice about worrying for the future:

> *'Therefore do not worry about tomorrow, for tomorrow will worry about itself. Each day has enough trouble of its own.'*
> (Matthew 6:34 NIV)

I know all too well that it is not easy to stop worrying about things of the past, present or future (particularly if this is a personal weakness, as it was for me), but it takes discipline and a continual focussing on God (see chapter 3 – Let the peace of God). In the verse of scripture quoted above, Jesus said, *'do **not** worry'* – that is a clear word of instruction, in fact it is a command; this is why we must make every endeavour not to worry and to take authority over those out-of-control and disturbing thoughts, with the authority that Jesus gave to all His followers.

There is a tremendous verse of scripture written by the apostle Paul that has encouraged me to believe that my thoughts can come under the control and authority of my Lord and Saviour, Jesus:

> *'Casting down imaginations, and every high thing that exalteth itself against the knowledge of God, and bringing into captivity every thought to the obedience of Christ;'*
> (2 Corinthians 10:5 KJV)

There have been times when I have felt that my thoughts have been out of control, almost as if my mind has been rushing about trying to find something to latch onto, something that I could worry about. Yet Paul's words in this verse have made me realise that these fearful worrying thoughts, these *'imaginations'*, which have at times overtaken the *'knowledge of God'* in me, need to be cast down and made captive and subject to the authority of Jesus. Fear and worry should no longer rule me, but with the authority of Jesus I should have control over them.

The words in the last verse of the song say:
'All the time I know God is with me...'
It is almost incomprehensible to think that the one and only God should want to commune with us, His children; after all, He is the almighty Creator and we are simply part of His creation – yet the contents of Bible proves that, time and time again, He has desired not to have dominance and control over His children, but to have fellowship with them, leading them into His perfect ways. I have no doubt of God's constant presence in my life (He resides within the heart of every believer by the Holy Spirit), and the knowledge of this brings such a feeling of security. I know that taking the positive action to entrust my life completely into God's hands, results in a true and lasting peace and sense of freedom and liberty.

> *'Stand fast therefore in the liberty wherewith Christ hath made us free, and be not entangled again with the yoke of bondage.'*
> (Galatians 5:1 KJV)

I totally agree with Paul as he encouraged the church at Galatia to *'Stand fast therefore in the liberty wherewith Christ hath made us free...'* and not to be *'...entangled again with the yoke of bondage.'* Who in their right minds would want to go back into bondage, when they had experienced freedom – I certainly wouldn't – but it isn't always that easy and will more often than not, require us to *'Stand fast..',* to have a determination and perseverance in holding onto God, not letting go.

Anyone who has been spiritually bound (whether it be by fear, depression, anxiety, sin or anything else which has seemingly interrupted their walk with God), would know how terrible it feels; but in my case it severely restricted me from freely worshipping God, as I was often drawn into myself and felt unable (or so it seemed) to enter into worship and praise. Therefore, the words in the last verse of the song which say, **'I'm free to enter His glorious presence; free from care and free from sin'**, are truly heartfelt.

I am sure I am not alone in having experienced times of feeling restricted in worshipping God – perhaps not everybody has felt this for the same reasons I have shared – but there may have been times (even if brief or infrequent), when problems or situations have preoccupied our thoughts, or perhaps at times we have felt that we are simply not 'in the right frame of mind' to worship; but the truth of the matter is that feelings come and go, they change so readily and because of this, they should not rule our actions or prevent us from worshipping God (either on our own or corporately with others), for God never changes and is always worthy of honour and glory. However, not only is worshipping God the right and proper thing to do, but if done with a sincere heart, I believe that true worship lifts our spirits and we also are blessed. In the church I attended for 16 years, there were times when I and the other believers who were there, experienced heartfelt worship, when we put everything else aside and simply poured out our love, thanks and adoration to God. During these precious times in God's presence I was truly blessed as my heart felt full of God's love and power.

What a great privilege for us, who are the children of God, to be allowed to enter into the presence of the almighty, all powerful and holy God; I feel that sometimes we need to let the reality of this great honour permeate our being so that we can appreciate it more. Of course, by our own efforts we could never have gained the right to come into God's presence – but as the following verses affirm, the way into God's presence has been made open for us by the precious shed blood of Jesus – it is the only way.

'Having therefore, brethren, boldness to enter into the holiest by the blood of Jesus,
By a new and living way, which he hath consecrated for us, through the veil, that is to say, his flesh;
And having an high priest over the house of God;
Let us draw near with a true heart in full assurance of faith, having our hearts sprinkled from an evil conscience, and our bodies washed with pure water.' (Hebrews 10:19-22 KJV)

If I could count the number of hours, days, weeks or even months of my life that I have spent on fear and worry, anxiety and depression, I am sure I would be horrified at the waste of time; but rather than causing me to waste any more time by considering regrets, this should spur me on to live my life with a different attitude – not worrying about the past, present or future, but living with an awareness of God's constant presence in my life.

If I live every day of my life in the knowledge that God is always the same – He never changes – then whatever things I might have to face, whatever today or tomorrow might bring, I know that I will be able to proclaim that:

'This is a day to praise the Lord.'

This is a day of celebration.
This is a day to worship God.
This is a day of jubilation;
And this is a day to praise the Lord!

I won't worry about the past;
From condemnation Christ set me free!
I have been given a brand new life;
I live in Christ and Christ in me.

This is a day of celebration....

I won't worry about the future,
For it has enough cares of its own.
I will centre my thoughts on Jesus,
My peace is found in Him alone.

This is a day of celebration....

All the time I know God is with me,
And I freely can worship Him;
I'm free to enter His glorious presence;
Free from care and free from sin.

This is a day of celebration....

CHAPTER 21

God is mighty, strong to save

There has been a recurring theme throughout this book which is a representation of the many times in my life when I have struggled with fear, anxiety and depression. My intention in writing so much about this subject is not to bring undeserved attention to the devil (who I believe has been at the root of these attacks), but it is my hope that in giving an honest account of what I have been through, along with the revelations which I believe God gave in order to strengthen me, I will bring glory to God; I also hope that anyone who is struggling in the same way I did, will be encouraged to turn to God for help because He is faithful, true to His Word and loves His children.

The song **'God is mighty, strong to save'** was inspired at yet another time when I believe God wanted to reaffirm within my heart, truth from His Word; this time, the revelation came from words written by David the Psalmist in Psalm 18:1-32. In particular, my attention was drawn to the way that God reacted when David had come under attack from his enemies and then delivered him from them. As I read the account of this in Psalm 18, I actually had a feeling of excitement as I had the assurance in my spirit that what God did for David, He would do for me too, because I am also His child.

When reading accounts within the Bible of how God has protected and delivered His children from the attacking enemy, I have found it helpful at times to relate their situation to my own (particularly when I have felt like I am spiritually, mentally or physically under attack). It is in believing that God never changes that I am encouraged to put my trust in Him, believing He will work on my behalf and deliver me from the enemy, just as He did in times past.

When I consider David the Psalmist, I recognise that during his lifetime he wrote many beautiful, heartfelt words both about God and to God – sometimes rejoicing or praising and sometimes crying out in despair – his words were honest and I think this why I have often been able to identify with them.

The words of Psalm 18 were written by David after a particular time in his life, when having come under attack by his enemies, God worked marvellously on his behalf to deliver him. The following words which precede the Psalm provide us with a succinct summary, outlining the very basics of the story to give us insight and understanding:

> 'To the chief Musician, A Psalm of David, the servant of the LORD who spake unto the LORD the words of this song in the day that the LORD delivered him from the hand of all his enemies, and from the hand of Saul...'
>
> (Psalm 18 Introduction prior to first verse KJV)

In Psalm 18, David not only told of the attacks from his enemies and the effect they had on him, but also in a wonderful way, David used beautifully descriptive words to reflect God's attributes; he certainly proved his depth of feeling toward God in the way he expressed all that God meant to him. I don't believe that the symbolism David used in describing God's attributes were just empty, meaningless words, and it is evident from the way he wrote, that David wasn't describing a God who was distant from him; no – I believe that God's attributes encompassed David's life and became a living reality for him as he experienced them first hand in his own situation, where he was facing real trials. It was because David had a personal relationship with God, and was experiencing God's touch upon his life that he could proclaim God as:

- '*my strength*'
- '*my rock,*'
- '*my fortress*'
- '*my deliverer;*'
- '*my shield*'
- '*the horn of my salvation*'
- '*my stronghold*'

'The LORD is my rock, my fortress and my deliverer; my God is my rock, in whom I take refuge. He is my shield and the horn of my salvation, my stronghold.' (Psalm 18:2 NIV)

I believe it is good to declare the greatness and power of God in both prayer and praise; it is not that God needs to be reminded of His own greatness (although it is right that we honour Him by proclaiming it), but I believe that when we have a personal revelation of His attributes, confessing these truths helps to combat negativity. Negativity is something which the devil has often tried to plant in my mind (such as negative, self critical, self condemning thoughts about myself or my situation), but God wants our minds to be filled with a greater knowledge of Him; and I am certain that this helps us to trust Him more (see Ephesians 1:17-21).

As I continued to read Psalm 18, I found that I was able to identify with David as he so vividly described his feelings when he came under attack:

'The cords of death entangled me; the torrents of destruction overwhelmed me. The cords of the grave coiled around me; the snares of death confronted me.' (Psalm 18:4-5 NIV)

The attacks I had been under were from an unseen enemy (the devil) and were spiritual ones, whereas I believe that David's attack was a physical one; however, his words struck a chord in my heart as I likened them to my experience of suffering fear and anxiety. For those who have never experienced such an attack in the mind, it might seem that likening David's experience (as he described it in Psalm 18:4-5) to a non-physical attack such as fear and anxiety, seems somewhat melodramatic; but anyone who has felt the desperation that can come with these things, as I have done, will understand how I was able to identify with David's words.

During the many times in my life when I have come 'under attack', it has helped me when I have recognised who is responsible for it. In the Bible, Peter makes it clear who our enemy is:

> *'Be sober, be vigilant; because your adversary the devil, as a roaring lion, walketh about, seeking whom he may devour:'*
> (1 Peter 5:8 KJV)

Our enemy (or *'adversary'* as Peter named it), is not flesh and blood, but rather, the enemy of our souls – the devil; but the great truth is that God is stronger than this enemy! When we fully grasp this truth, what assurance it gives us; but what is equally reassuring and amazing is the knowledge that this great God loves us like a perfect father, who with care and concern listens to our heart's cry when we are in distress:

> *'In my distress I called to the LORD; I cried to my God for help. From his temple he heard my voice; my cry came before him, into his ears.'*
> (Psalm 18:6 NIV)

There have been many times in my life when full of anxiety and being in distress (just like David) I have called out to God in despair. As I read David's words they really made an impression on me and brought me comfort to know that even from His *'temple'*, God is not cut off from us, He is not distant, but He hears our cry. However, as much as that truth was impressed on me, what made a greater impact and amazed me, was God's reaction to the attacks against David:

> *'The earth trembled and quaked, and the foundations of the mountains shook; they trembled because he was angry.'*
> (Psalm 18:7 NIV)

What insight we are given into God's character when we read that He was actually angry because the one He loved was being attacked; He expressed His justifiable anger on the earth by using the elements, but then went on to respond on behalf of David by taking action to protect him and rescue him from his foes:

> *'Out of the brightness of his presence clouds advanced, with hailstones and bolts of lightning. The LORD thundered from heaven; the voice of the Most High resounded. He shot his arrows and scattered the enemies, great bolts of lightning and routed them.'* (Psalm 18:12-14 NIV)

> *'He reached down from on high and took hold of me; he drew me out of deep waters. He rescued me from my powerful enemy, from my foes, who were too strong for me. They confronted me in the day of my disaster, but the LORD was my support. He brought me out into a spacious place; he rescued me because he delighted in me.'* (Psalm 18:16-19 NIV)

Whilst I read and re-read the words of Psalm 18, I believe God confirmed in my spirit that the truths within it (which showed how He responded to David's distress and moved on his behalf), would also be true for me in those times when I came under attack and was in distress. Praise God that He is unchangeable and is faithful to His children! However, there is an important part within the Psalm which mustn't be overlooked or excluded, where David recognises the fact that God was faithful to him because he had been faithful to God and kept true to His ways:

> *'To the faithful you show yourself faithful...'* (Psalm 18:25a NIV)

> *'The LORD has dealt with me according to my righteousness; according to the cleanness of my hands he has rewarded me. For I have kept the ways of the LORD; I have not done evil by turning from my God. All his laws are before me; I have not turned away from his decrees. I have been blameless before him and have kept myself from sin.'* (Psalm 18:20-23 NIV)

It is evident from David's words (and I recognise myself), that to come under God's protection I need to be faithful to Him, endeavouring to live my life according to His Word; I need to live a righteous, *'blameless'* life and be *'free from sin'*. However, knowing how I sometimes fail God and fall into sin, I realise that it is not possible for me to accomplish these things on my own, but it is possible through Christ Jesus and through His precious blood; therefore I gratefully receive the continual cleansing of the blood of Jesus over my life.

The song **'God is mighty, strong to save'**, is not a paraphrase of Psalm 18 – but has been inspired greatly by it. It is a response to the revelation which God gave to me. God loves us more than we could ever imagine and I believe that He doesn't only help us in spiritual matters, but He provides tangible help when we face any types of trials and difficulties – not always instantly or in the way that we think is right, but in His perfect timing and in the way He chooses. One thing is certain, in those times when we come under attack from the evil one, we can rest assured that we are (as the song says), **'safe and secure'** in God's hands.

NB. I have only quoted a few specific verses from Psalm 18 but I can highly recommend reading the whole of it for your own encouragement and blessing. I trust that God will reveal the truths contained within it to your heart, as He did for me.

God is mighty, strong to save;
He's my rock, I trust in Him.
When to Him, my life I gave,
He rescued me from the power of sin.
We wrestle not with flesh and blood,
But powers and principalities;
But God is mightier than the foe,
And I know that He cares for me....

For He reached down from Heaven
And He lifted me up.
It's so wonderful to know
That He saw my distress and He heard my cry
And He rescued me from the foe.
For He lifted me up out of deep waters.
He lifted me up so I could stand on the solid rock.
Thank You Lord,
I'm safe and secure in Your hands.

CHAPTER 22

Reminders at Christmas time

'Jesus is the reason for the season'. This motto is one that is probably fairly well known among Christians, but I believe now more than ever, the truth of it needs to be upheld by the followers of Christ, not only in the way that we celebrate Christmas ourselves, but also in the way that we show this to the world. It saddens me to know that so often the season of Christmas is celebrated without any reference to the Person, who is the only true reason for the season; even the seemingly minor practice of abbreviating 'Happy Christmas' to 'Happy Xmas', excludes Christ, when He should be the central theme. I believe that in all of our Christmas celebrations, we should keep our focus on our Lord and Saviour – Jesus.

The song, **'Reminders at Christmas time'** looks at some of the familiar traditions of Christmas and how even in them, our thoughts can be turned towards Jesus.

'Presents given to each other'
It is a precious moment when, having carefully and lovingly chosen a Christmas gift for a loved one, we give that gift to them; what satisfaction and enjoyment it brings to us, as they open the gift with joy. On the other hand, it is also a precious moment when we receive a gift that has been given with such love and careful thought. How much more wonderful to recognise and receive the gift which God the Father gave to mankind – His own Son Jesus, who was given as a baby, but grew to a man and gave His life for us – this gift was carefully considered and planned by God.

> *'For God so loved the world, that he gave his only begotten Son, that whosoever believeth in him should not perish, but have everlasting life.'* (John 3:16 KJV)

God gave us a most wonderful and precious gift – Jesus; this truth is not only cause for celebration and rejoicing, but more importantly, for proclamation to the world; and we who know Him as Saviour and Lord, must do this.

'Carol Singing in the churches'

Singing Christmas carols is a great tradition, but because we have sung many of them countless times before, I feel there is a danger of singing the words 'parrot fashion'; failing to take in, or rejoice in the truths contained within them (truths which are mainly based on scripture). It would be good if we could sing these inspired songs as if they were brand new to us, so that we would take heed of the words and truly rejoice in them.

> *'And suddenly there was with the angel a multitude of the heavenly host praising God, and saying, Glory to God in the highest, and on earth peace, good will toward men.'* (Luke 2:13-14 KJV)

When Jesus was born, there were multitudes of angels who rejoiced and praised God over the little town of Bethlehem; so how much more should we rejoice because not only do we remember that God came to earth as a baby, but know that He is now Lord of all and King of kings, and if we receive Him as such (as Saviour, Lord and King), then we can be reconciled to God and have peace with Him.

'Candles in the darkness burning'

There is something attractive and fascinating about a candle flickering in the darkness, and although the flame may be small, it can seem to bring a sense of warmth and cosiness as its light eliminates the darkness within a room. Of course, the light seems to shine more brightly when it shines in a dark place – and this is how Jesus is wonderfully portrayed in the Bible – as *'light'* shining in the *'darkness'*– both by John, a disciple of Jesus and by Jesus Himself:

> *'In him was life, and that life was the light of men. The light shines in the darkness, but the darkness has not understood it....The true light that gives light to every man was coming into the world.'* (John 1:4-5&9 NIV)

> *'When Jesus spoke again to the people, he said, "I am the light of the world. Whoever follows me will never walk in darkness, but will have the light of life."'* (John 8:12 NIV)

Sometimes children are afraid of the dark and they like to lighten the darkness with perhaps even the smallest of lights (such as a night light, or the glimmer of light through a slightly open bedroom door) and this gives them reassurance and a feeling of security. In a spiritual sense, the same could be said for mankind – that without Jesus in our lives, we live in spiritual darkness, but with Jesus, He brings His glorious light, which not only lightens our darkness and gives us security, but if we allow His life to enter ours, His light radiates from us, so that others can see He lives within us.

The world at large may not recognise the true reason for celebrating Christmas, but I believe that the children of God, who have received Jesus as Saviour and Lord, must ensure that Jesus is at the centre of every Christmas celebration.

Let's celebrate because:
We recognise the great love God had for us in giving His only Son, Jesus – the most precious gift.

Let's celebrate because:
Our lives can overflow with joy as we rejoice in the fact that Jesus came to earth; but what greater celebration and rejoicing is ours once we have received Jesus as our Saviour.

Let's celebrate because:
> We recognise that Jesus is the light of the world, and the light which radiates from Him can illumine our lives also, if we receive Him into our hearts.

The song finishes with the line, **'This Christmas, worship Christ the King!'** Of course we do not have to be limited (and we should not only be limited) to celebrating at Christmas time, the fact that Jesus came to earth; let's rejoice and give Him praise all the year through, for He is worthy of our continual adoration!

Presents given to each other,
Reminding us at Christmas time,
That God, our loving heavenly Father,
Gave a gift so rare and fine;
He gave His one and only Son,
A gift of love for me.
Receive this gift with thankful heart
And then the truth you'll see,
That Christ, the Saviour of the world,
Was babe and yet divine.
Let's celebrate this Christmas time.

Carol singing in the churches,
Reminding us at Christmas time,
Of angels singing songs of praises,
Telling of the wondrous sign,
That Jesus came to earth from Heaven,
Not as mighty King,
But as a helpless, humble babe,
His praises we should sing;
For Jesus is now Lord of all,
Receive Him while you may,
Give thanks to Him on Christmas day.

Candles in the darkness burning,
Reminding us at Christmas time,
That Jesus Christ, the light from Heaven
Came on this dark earth to shine.
So let His light shine in your heart,
Let darkness fade away;
His light will bring a bright new hope,
He'll turn your night to day.
Let others see His light in you,
Proclaim Him as your King
And make Him Lord of everything.

This Christmas, worship Christ the King!

CHAPTER 23

A promise through the ages

Throughout history there have been individuals who have made a tremendous impact on a great many people, some for the good and some for bad; but there was one who's coming to earth changed everything for all eternity – and His Name is Jesus.

A little while before Christmas one year I was seeking God for a new song that I could sing during the Carol Service at the church I attended. I believe that in response to my seeking, God predominantly filled my mind with the words, **'For He came – the promised Messiah'**.

The coming of Jesus into the world wasn't an accident – far from it – for it was planned by God and was promised to mankind; it was His response to our need of salvation. Prior to the birth of Jesus, God chose specific people to make known this promise of hope – this promise of the coming Messiah – Jesus, who was God's own Son. One of the prophets who foretold His coming (approximately 700 years prior to the birth of Jesus), was Isaiah; he spoke the following God-given prophetic words concerning Jesus:

> *'For unto us a child is born, unto us a son is given: and the government shall be upon his shoulder: and his name shall be called Wonderful, Counsellor, The mighty God, The everlasting Father, The Prince of Peace.'* (Isaiah 9:6 KJV)

> *'All we like sheep have gone astray; we have turned every one to his own way; and the LORD hath laid on him the iniquity of us all.'* (Isaiah 53:6 KJV)

Sadly, it seems that in recent years there have been those who have disputed the miraculous aspects of the Bible and particularly regarding the virgin birth; but this is nothing new, for even Joseph (Mary's future husband) had difficulty at first, taking on board what Mary had told him, that even though she was a virgin, she would give birth to God's own son. Of course, it was understandable that Joseph might need reassurance of the truth, because the truth was totally unexpected and astounding; however, Joseph was an important part in God's plan, so to aid him in believing the truth, God sent an angel to him in a dream with a message about the promised Saviour, Jesus:

> '...Joseph, thou son of David, fear not to take unto thee Mary thy wife: for that which is conceived in her is of the Holy Ghost. And she shall bring forth a son, and thou shalt call his name JESUS: for he shall save his people from their sins.'
>
> (Matthew 1:20b-21 KJV)

These verses contain wonderful promises of hope for all those who would believe, and they are proof enough that God sent His Son for the benefit of all mankind; God looked ahead into the future, recognised our great need and out of love, gave us Jesus.

I don't believe that God only saw the faceless masses that needed someone to save them from their sin; I don't believe that He could only see sinners who had no identity – but I believe that God saw every individual. I am without doubt that God saw me in my sinful state and knew every sin that I would ever commit; I also believe that He knew how I would condemn myself when I became aware of my own failings and sin. How can I be sure of this? The answer is contained within God's Word, for there are many verses in the Bible about God's knowledge of us; this convinces me that God not only knows my every thought and action, but that He knows them before they have even taken place.

The Psalmist wrote these words:

> *'O LORD, you have searched me and you know me. You know when I sit and when I rise; you perceive my thoughts from afar. You discern my going out and my lying down; you are familiar with all my ways. Before a word is on my tongue you know it completely, O LORD.'* (Psalm 139:1-4 NIV)

Paul wrote about God's foreknowledge of us:

> *'For those God foreknew he also predestined to be conformed to the likeness of his Son...'* (Romans 8:29a NIV)

When I consider the fact that even though God knew everything about me (including my past, present and future sins), He still gave the best thing He had (Jesus) to save me from my sin, my heart is filled with overwhelming gratitude and love.

As I have an assurance within my heart of God's love for me and have known His help and intervention in my life, I sometimes wonder how people manage when they leave God out of their lives – how they cope without God when faced with difficult situations. Of course, I realise that God gave all of mankind a free will, whereby each one can freely decide to accept Him, or reject Him. Not only have I personally experienced what it is like to accept God's presence into my life, (feeling the joy and peace He gives, as well as His strength and support in the difficult times), but I have also experienced times when, for one reason or another (usually because of depression or fear), I have foolishly turned away from God for a while. Through all of my experiences I can say with certainty that I would not want to live my life without God's presence in it.

But just consider for a moment what questions might remain unanswered if God hadn't responded to the world's need of a saviour, if Jesus had not **'left all the glory of Heaven'** and come to earth?

- How would I (a sinner, separated from God because of my sin) be able to have peace and reconciliation with God?

- How could I be saved from the eternal punishment in Hell, which I deserve because of my sin?
- How could I have the promise of everlasting life?
- In a world that is increasingly filled with despair and confusion, how could I ever have peace of mind, or any hope for the future?

The fact is, without Jesus, I would have no hope, I would be devoid of peace and lost for eternity; but the wonderful truth is that **'He came'**. Jesus was God's answer to our greatest need; this was His plan of salvation for mankind.

Because this song was written for Christmas, it encourages that at Christmas time, we should **'remember that Jesus came as fulfilment of God's plan'** and **'give Him...praises'**, but of course, Christmas is just one season of the year and we must remember Him and praise Him every day of the year. However, I do believe that as we celebrate the season of Christmas, we have a wonderful opportunity to share with those who have not yet grasped the truth of why Jesus came to earth.

The fulfilment of God's promise when Jesus came to the earth cannot be ignored – it requires a response from every person; as the song says:

**'So just believe His love for you, receive Him while you may,
And you will know a blessed sweet release'.**

A promise through the ages
Had been given by God to man,
That to our world a Saviour would come.
For man had drifted far from God
When sin had entered in;
Then Jesus came,
The precious promised One.

For He came…
The promised Messiah.
And He came…
The hope of all the earth.
Yet He came…
Leaving all of His glory;
In a stable was His humble birth.

For He left all the glory of Heaven,
Because God had a heart of love for man.
And at Christmas time, let's remember
That Jesus came as fulfilment of God's plan -
Redeeming plan.
For He came…
The promised Messiah.
And one day He'll come to earth again;
Not as babe in a poor humble stable,
But as great mighty King come to reign.

When Jesus comes into your heart
He'll take your sin away,
He'll give you joy that lasts
And perfect peace.
So just believe His love for you,
Receive Him while you may,
And you will know a blessèd sweet release.

For He came...
The promised Messiah.
Prince of peace,
And Jesus was His Name.
So at Christmas give Him your praises,
And rejoice in your heart that He came...
That Jesus came...
I'm so glad He came.

CHAPTER 24

We're in the presence of the King

There are a great many promises contained within the Bible, which is God's Word to man; and these promises are a source of encouragement and blessing to His children. One such promise was given by Jesus Himself, as He was teaching His disciples:

> 'For where two or three are gathered together in my name, there am I in the midst of them.' (Matthew 18:20 KJV)

How wonderful to know that when we come together with other believers, whether in a church, or house-group, or just in an informal setting – Jesus has promised that if we are gathered in His Name, then He will be present. Remember that the prophet Isaiah, when foretelling the birth of Jesus, said that He would be called '*Immanuel*', meaning, '*God with us*' (See Isaiah 7:14 KJV and Matthew 1:23 KJV). I wonder if we always realise the truth of this promise, this fact that Jesus is actually with us.

If we believe that Jesus is with us as we gather together, then surely we must act accordingly. An example that we often considered during times of worship in the church I attended, was how we would react if the monarch of our nation came into the church – surely this would affect everything that we did; how we would act, speak and dress. It would be fitting for us to give honour and respect to royalty; but how much more then, should we give honour and respect to the ultimate royalty, who is King of kings and Lord of lords.

In the book of Revelation in the Bible, we read of how John the apostle had a revelation about Jesus and of future events. During this time he had first hand witness of the heavenly worship of Jesus – the Lamb of God:

> *'Then I looked and heard the voice of many angels, numbering thousands upon thousands, and ten thousand times ten thousand. They encircled the throne and the living creatures and the elders. In a loud voice they sang: "Worthy is the Lamb, who was slain, to receive power and wealth and wisdom and strength and honour and glory and praise!"'*
> (Revelation 5:11-12 NIV)

The song, **'We're in the presence of the King'**, reflects my heart in desiring to give Jesus His rightful position, either when I worship together with fellow believers, or in those solitary times when I am worshipping Him alone.

I believe that it is the Holy Spirit within us who helps us to worship Jesus, for He reveals within our hearts, the truth of who Jesus is – His authority and His position (given to Him by His Father, God); the apostle Paul reveals this, as he writes a letter to the Church at Philippi:

> *'Therefore God exalted him to the highest place and gave him the name that is above every name,'* (Philippians 2:9 NIV)

As we draw near to God in closer communion – as we recognise the awesome sacrifice that Jesus made to purchase our salvation – as we recognise the truth that we don't worship a dead God, but One who was raised from death to life – then our love for Him deepens and we want to worship Him, not only for what He has done (which naturally we want to do), but also for who He is. I must say that any time when I have been in a place of worship, where there hasn't been reverence for the Lord, I have not only recognised this, but felt grieved in my spirit (which I am sure is because the Holy Spirit, who can be grieved, is present within my heart – see Ephesians 4:30).

If anyone doubted that God understands us and understands what we go through in life, the fact that Jesus came to earth as a man and lived on earth in a human body (even making friends with the lowliest of people), should help in realising that He is fully able to identify with us and us with Him; but this fact should never make us forget that although Jesus was fully man, He was also fully God and is God, and therefore should be honoured and respected as God.

I was reminded of Moses, who was tending a flock of sheep in the desert, when an angel appeared to him in the flames of fire from within a bush. Moses was curious and wanted to take a closer look, because although there were flames, the bush was not destroyed by them. Up until that point, the day had probably been just another ordinary day for Moses, as he looked after the sheep; he was in a dusty desert place, probably not much different from any other desert place he had been, but this time it became a holy place because God was there and spoke to him:

> 'When the LORD saw that he had gone over to look, God called to him from within the bush, "Moses! Moses!" And Moses said, "Here I am." "Do not come any closer," God said. "Take off your sandals, for the place where you are standing is holy ground."'
>
> (Exodus 3:4-5 NIV)

I believe that when we spend time in worship, when we meet together in Jesus' Name, we stand on holy ground, for God Himself is there. I love to worship God and know His presence, but sometimes there are external situations that would try to fill my mind as I come into a time of worship; however, I know that when I lay these things aside and devote myself and my time to true worship of my Lord, I am certain to be blessed in His presence – and I believe this is true for all those who worship Him with sincerity of heart.

Jesus is worthy of all honour and praise, for He is, and for all eternity will be, the King of kings and Lord of Lords; and as such, He should receive all our respect and reverence.

**'Lord, we honour You and give the glory due,
Son of God, eternal King.'**

We're in the presence of the King.
Lift up your voice and praises sing.
This place is holy, for He's here.
Come bow in reverence and fear;
For King Jesus, You are great beyond compare,
Like a jewel that is precious, yet so rare.
Lord, we honour You and give the glory due;
Son of God, eternal King.

CHAPTER 25

I hear the sound of heavy rain

On the day of Pentecost, when the Holy Spirit was poured out on all the believers, the apostle Peter stood in front of a baffled and scoffing crowd and quoted these words, which many years earlier had been spoken by the prophet Joel:

> 'And it shall come to pass in the last days, saith God, I will pour out of my Spirit upon all flesh: and your sons and your daughters shall prophesy, and your young men shall see visions, and your old men shall dream dreams:
> And on my servants and on my handmaidens I will pour out in those days of my Spirit; and they shall prophesy:
> And I will shew wonders in heaven above, and signs in the earth beneath; blood, and fire, and vapour of smoke:
> The sun shall be turned into darkness, and the moon into blood, before that great and notable day of the Lord come:'
>
> (Acts 2:17-20 KJV)

The annual Jewish festival of Pentecost had been celebrated many times before, but for the apostles and other believers, who had heeded the instruction from Jesus to stay in Jerusalem and wait for the gift His Father had promised, this particular day of Pentecost was one which would be different from all those preceding it. It was the apostle Peter who made the connection between what was taking place on this specific day of Pentecost to Joel's prophecy and he recognised that he was seeing the start of the prophecy's fulfilment; for the Holy Spirit had been poured out upon the believers and they were in the time of the *'last days'*.

Of course, many years have passed since Peter spoke those words, but I believe that we are now living in the last of the *'last days'*. Earlier in this book (chapters 15 and 16) I wrote about some of the prophecies that refer to the Last Days and what we will see taking place on the earth (such as wars, earthquakes, famine, along with the attitudes in the hearts of mankind); but before the Lord Jesus returns I believe that we will see God's power come upon Holy Spirit filled believers, we will see signs and wonders in the natural world and an end time revival which will bring in a great harvest of souls (saving those dear ones from eternal damnation **1).

**1 I believe that there are only two eternal destinations for mankind – Heaven and Hell – they are real places (see Matthew 13:24-30, 36-52 and John 14:1-4). Bible teaching is very clear that the day will come when every soul will be judged and sent to one place or the other – Heaven or Hell (which is sometimes referred to in the Bible as the lake of fire, or fiery furnace); but God's desire is that none should perish (which would mean being separated from Him forever in Hell,) – Jesus said, *'Even so it is not the will of your Father which is in heaven, that one of these little ones should perish.'* (Matthew 18:14 KJV)

The song, **'I hear the sound of heavy rain'** came at a time when I was being very encouraged and blessed by a move of God's Holy Spirit which was taking place not only in the church world wide, but also within the church I was attending (which comprised of just a small group of believers, yet God's presence was tangible in our midst). I was drawn to a particular account in the Old Testament of the Bible about God's servant, Elijah (recorded in 1 Kings 16:29-18:46). At that time the king of Israel was Ahab; he provoked God to anger not only by doing much evil in His sight, but also by worshipping Baal, a false God (see 1 Kings 16:29-33).

God sent a message to Ahab through Elijah, who bravely spoke the following prophetic words to the King:

'...As the LORD God of Israel liveth, before whom I stand, there shall not be dew nor rain these years, but according to my word.' (1 Kings 17:1b KJV)

After Elijah had confronted King Ahab with this promise, which would bring about such catastrophe in Ahab's kingdom, Elijah had to flee from him and spent much time in hiding, as God instructed him. Many other prophets of the Lord also had to go into hiding during that time and they were helped by a man called Obadiah, who although was in charge of Ahab's palace, still remained faithful to God.

In the third year of the drought, the word of the Lord came once again to Elijah, instructing him to go back to Ahab, for He was once again going to send rain upon the land. It would naturally have been a fearsome thing for Elijah to meet with Ahab, but Elijah showed true faith in the living God and was undeterred by the threat of danger. This was the time for Elijah to prove to Ahab (along with the prophets of Baal) once and for all, that his God was the only true and living God.

Elijah finally met with Ahab and boldly confronted him. Ahab, the prophets of Baal and all the people who had turned away from the Lord needed to be challenged as to who they should follow – Baal, or the God of Elijah. It was agreed that both Elijah and the prophets of Baal would call on their gods and whichever god answered by sending fire onto the altar, would be proved to be the real and true God.

Of course, the outcome was that Elijah's God, was proven to be the true God, because He answered Elijah's plea by sending fire upon the altar (this being all the more evident that the fire was from God, not man, because Elijah had previously ordered the altar to be saturated with water). The people were greatly affected by the display of God's mighty power and it resulted in them recognising who was indeed the true God:

'And when all the people saw it, they fell on their faces: and they said, The LORD, he is the God; the LORD, he is the God.'
(1 Kings 18:39 KJV)

As inspiring as this part of the story is, the part which actually inspired the song, **'I hear the sound of heavy rain'**, was concerning the long awaited rain (which as you may recall, wouldn't fall until Elijah declared it). Of course, I had to share the first part of the story to enable me to share what followed in the second part – the part that spoke to me.

Although naturally speaking, there was no sign of the long awaited rain, Elijah had an inward assurance that rain was on its way and in fact, spoke in faith as if it was a foregone conclusion:

> *'And Elijah said unto Ahab, Get thee up, eat and drink; for there is a sound of abundance of rain.'* (1 Kings 18:41 KJV)

Elijah sent his servant to go and look out to the sea, but the servant came back and said that that there was nothing. Elijah instructed him to go back again and again; but not until the seventh time did the servant come back with news of the first small sign – a little cloud – giving indication that it might rain:

> *'And it came to pass at the seventh time, that he said, Behold, there ariseth a little cloud out of the sea, like a man's hand. And he said, Go up, say unto Ahab, Prepare thy chariot, and get thee down, that the rain stop thee not. And it came to pass in the mean while, that the heaven was black with clouds and wind, and there was a great rain. And Ahab rode, and went to Jezreel.'*
> (1 Kings 18:44-45 KJV)

I believe the Holy Spirit led me to this passage of scripture to show me that in just the same way Elijah had an inward witness and held firm onto the belief that rain was already on its way, we too with conviction, should hold onto the inward witness that God places in our hearts regarding the coming 'rain of the Holy Spirit'; we may see only a tiny sign (like a small cloud) to indicate the ensuing revival, signs, wonders and power of God being displayed in greater measure on the earth – perhaps we see no signs as yet where we are, but have received an inward witness in our spirit (which has been given by God's Holy Spirit) that the move of God is already on the way.

I had found great encouragement in what the Lord was doing at the time of writing this song, but I believe every Christian should be encouraged, not only when we see the move of God's Holy Spirit (wherever and whenever it takes place), but also when God gives an assurance in our hearts that He is moving; in all these things, we should rejoice and continue to pray in faith, believing that God will bring about His plans and purposes in all the earth, including the place where we are.

I hear the sound of heavy rain,
It's coming! It's coming!
Look for the signs, have faith again,
I know it' coming soon.
The thirsty land will be revived
When the rain comes, the rain comes.
Just see the cloud; the rain is on its way.

We've prayed for the rain
To come on our land;
The rain of God's Spirit to pour down.
We've prayed for revival to touch the hearts of all;
It's started – there's raindrops all around!

I hear the sound of heavy rain...

And God will provide!
The rain – it will fall;
He'll pour out upon the thirsty ground.
The rain will refresh, the rain will revive;
And new life will spring up all around.

I hear the sound of heavy rain...

Yes, God's latter rain has started to fall,
We know He is moving in this place.
He's touched us with His power,
He's touched us with His love,
He's been right here with us by His grace.

We thank You Lord,
Make us vessels now for You,
That in all we do and say,
Others will see only You.

CHAPTER 26

Lord Jesus, I am so amazed

After I was made redundant in December 2008 from my job of 24 years, I felt I had a God-given opportunity to spend some of my newfound available time alone with Him and start to compile this book; although I was unsure of my long-term future or what direction God would lead me in, I felt that for the moment, I was doing what God wanted me to do.

As I was alone with God one day and spending some time in worship, a new song began to come into my mind; it started with the words, **'Lord Jesus, I am so amazed'** and it continued to speak of what it cost my Lord to sacrifice His life.

When I think of all the things that God has revealed to me over the years, I believe the greatest revelation concerns Jesus dying on the cross at Calvary; this is the foundation of the Christian faith and for those who would believe, it is the place of redemption, forgiveness and salvation. No-one who is truly born again can brush aside this great truth – that Jesus died for them – it is a personal and powerful experience for every individual who has received salvation; and I know that my life can only be lived in the light of this tremendous event.

It must be realised and acknowledged that the price for our salvation was costly to Jesus, for not only did He suffer great physical pain as He was scourged (whipped) – as the crown of thorns were placed upon Him, piercing His forehead – as He carried the cross on His already severely wounded back – as the nails were driven through His hands and feet – and as He hung on the cross, gasping for every breath – but also, there was another type of suffering which He endured. This suffering was the mental anguish which I believe He must have experienced as He witnessed the hate in people's eyes as they mocked Him, as they taunted Him and as they cried, *'Crucify him'*.

'Pilate therefore, willing to release Jesus, spake again to them. But they cried, saying, Crucify him, crucify him.'
(Luke 23:20-21 KJV)

'And when they had platted a crown of thorns, they put it upon his head, and a reed in his right hand: and they bowed the knee before him, and mocked him, saying, Hail, King of the Jews! And they spit upon him, and took the reed, and smote him on the head. And after that they had mocked him, they took the robe off from him, and put his own raiment on him, and led him away to crucify him.' (Matthew 27:29-31 KJV)

In the past, I have known what it feels like to have hurtful words spoken against me, sometimes hurting my feelings for a brief period, but in some cases, wounding me deeply for a greater length of time. I guess that I am not alone in my experience, as I am sure that many others have gone through varying degrees of hurt caused by unkind, untrue or undeserved words; but when I consider the fact that Jesus, who was God's own Son and had done no wrong, knew all that He would suffer (mentally as well as physically) and yet still chose to go to the cross, I am more greatly touched by this demonstration of great love.

David the Psalmist wrote the following words of praise to God and recognition of what his God was able to do:

'Bless the LORD, O my soul, and forget not all his benefits:'
(Psalm 103:2 KJV).

David knew it was good to remind himself of all that he had received from God; and I feel that we do a disservice to Jesus if we don't recognise or live in what He purchased by His sacrificial death on the cross and His resurrection from the dead.

- Jesus took all our sin:
  'But he was wounded for our transgressions, he was bruised for our iniquities...' (Isaiah 53:5a KJV)

- Jesus became our righteousness:
  'It is because of him that you are in Christ Jesus, who has become for us wisdom from God – that is, our righteousness, holiness and redemption.' (1 Corinthians 1:30 NIV)

- Salvation is received through Jesus:
  'For God did not appoint us to suffer wrath but to receive salvation through our Lord Jesus Christ.' (1 Thessalonians 5:9 NIV)

- Joy is ours through Jesus:
  'And not only so, but we also joy in God through our Lord Jesus Christ, by whom we have now received the atonement.' (Romans 5:11 KJV)

- Jesus received punishment to bring us peace:
  '...the punishment that brought us peace was upon him, and by his wounds we are healed.' (Isaiah 53:5b NIV)

- Victory is ours because Jesus was the victor over sin and death:
  'The sting of death is sin; and the strength of sin is the law. But thanks be to God, which giveth us the victory through our Lord Jesus Christ.' (1 Corinthians 15:56-57 KJV)

It is true that Jesus achieved all these things by His death and resurrection – He purchased them with His own blood – but we do not automatically receive them into our lives, for it requires our response – we must receive Jesus as our Saviour and Lord – then, these wonderful things can be ours; they were freely given and freely, we can receive.

I am not prone to having Godly dreams when I sleep, but I want to share one particular instance when I believe God gave me a specific revelation through a dream. I have tried to remember the detail of my dream as accurately as possible, and this is what I have recalled: I saw the cross of Calvary and although I am now unsure whether or not I saw Jesus on the cross (although I think He probably was), I know that I was there myself, nailed onto the cross. Then, whilst part of me (like a faded image of myself) remained nailed to the cross, the main part (the conscious, living part of me) dropped down from the cross onto the ground beneath. As I came from off the cross, I suddenly knew a complete release from fear and anxiety (which has oppressed and burdened my mind so often in the past); those things had been left on the cross and I felt a total freedom and a peace that I had never experienced before – I actually felt it! I experienced what it was like to have the feeling of total liberty; it was wonderful!

I knew that God was showing me that when Jesus was nailed to the cross, all my anxiety and fear was nailed there too; and through this I could attain perfect peace and freedom. What a tremendous revelation! Peace isn't something unachievable (as it had so often seemed to me), for Jesus paid the price so that I could receive it.

As I have considered all the Lord has done in my life (the spiritual revelations and truths He has shown me from God's Word, the help and strength He has given, but most importantly – how He gave His life and shed His precious blood for me at Calvary), I feel that I could write many words trying to express my thanks to Him; but even though they would be sincere and heartfelt, I know that words alone could not fully express my gratitude (as words can so often seem inadequate). It is true that God loves to hear our praises, but this is not all He desires, He doesn't just want 'lip service', He wants the whole of our lives; and this is echoed in the words of the song:

'So Lord, I give my heart to You, my love, my life, my all'.

I don't know what lies ahead for me in the future, but I hope that every step I take will be in accordance with God's preordained plan; and that out of love for my Lord, I will be totally committed to Him, knowing that He will be with me every step that I take.

> *'Now unto him that is able to keep you from falling, and to present you faultless before the presence of his glory with exceeding joy,*
> *To the only wise God our Saviour, be glory and majesty, dominion and power, both now and ever. Amen.'*
>
> (Jude 1:24-25 KJV)

Lord Jesus, I am so amazed
That though You were aware
Of all the suffering You'd endure,
The pain You'd have to bear;
And know the hate in people's eyes,
The hateful words they'd cry,
To know the pain You'd have to take –
An awesome sacrifice.
You knew full well the Father's plan,
Yet chose not to decline;
And this great act of love from You
Has touched my heart and mind.

Lord, I'm so glad You chose to take
This way of pain for me;
That You took all my sin and shame
When nailed upon that tree.
For You are now my righteousness,
Salvation and my joy,
My peace and my deliverance
From all that could destroy;
And death was not the end for You,
To life You rose again.
Your victory is my victory too,
If in You I remain.

My offering of gratitude in words,
Appears so small,
So Lord, I give my heart to You,
My love, my life, my all.

INSPIRED BY GOD – MUSIC

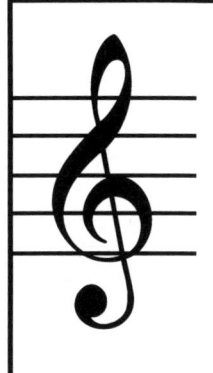

*'O sing unto the Lord
a new song:
sing unto the Lord,
all the earth.
Sing unto the Lord,
bless his name;
show forth his salvation
from day to day.'*

Psalm 96:1-2 (KJV)

1. All that I am

Annette Willis

♩ = 96

All that I am, all that I have, I offer unto You, my Saviour and my Lord. All anxieties, I lay them at the cross. O Lord, let me rest in You.

All that I am, all that I have, I offer unto You, my Saviour and my Lord. All my weaknesses, I lay them at the cross. O Lord, make me strong in You.

Words and Music: Copyright © Annette Willis

2. When I am alone

Annette Willis

♩ = 132

Verse 1

When I am alone and my thoughts begins to race, when my heart begins to feel the stress, I need that holy place; that place where I can meet with You and know the peace You give. Lord, I give my burdens all to You, You give me strength to live.

Chorus

Oh, Jesus, You're the Saviour of my soul. Loving Jesus, shed Your blood to make me whole. Precious

Words and music: Copyright © Annette Willis 2010

When I am alone... page 2

Saviour, gave Your life to set me free. You are living, hallelujah! Come and live Your life in me.

Verse 2
When I am confused and I don't know what to do, I just put my trust in You, O Lord, my friend who's ever true. In You there is security, I praise Your holy Name that yesterday, today, forever, Jesus, You're the same. Oh,

Words and music: Copyright © Annette Willis 2010

3. Let the peace of God

Annette Willis

Let the peace of God which sur-pass-es un-der-stand-ing, keep your hearts and minds through Je-sus Christ; so fix your gaze on Him, for He's our glor-ious Prince of peace. Al-ways put your trust in Him. Fo-cus on Je-sus; let no earth-ly thing dis-tract you. Fo-cus on Je-sus; He is

Words and music: Copyright © Annette Willis 2010

Let the peace of God... page 2

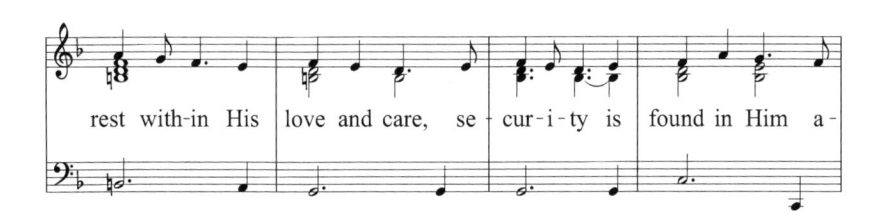

ev-'ry-thing you need. Let no prob-lem ov-er-whelm you, just rest with-in His love and care, se-cur-i-ty is found in Him a-lone.

Words and music: Copyright © Annette Willis 2010

4. Only the best for Jesus

Annette Willis

♩ = 138

Only the best for Jesus. Only the best for my King.
Only the best will I give Him as a daily offering; for He's done so very much for me, I want to give Him more... a life that's fully yielded, so that the Lord may pour His love and power in me, that others I may

Words and music: Copyright © Annette Willis 2010

Only the best for Jesus... page 2

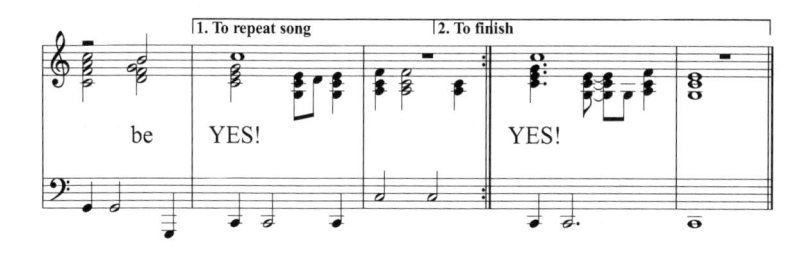

bless, what-ev-er He may ask of me, may my re-sponse

1. To repeat song

be YES!

2. To finish

YES!

Words and music: Copyright © Annette Willis 2010

5. In the power of His might, battles are won!

Annette Willis

♩ = 104

In the power of His might battles are won! In the power of His might I can stand! In the power of His might I know I am strong; when to Jesus Christ I belong.

Fine

1. .For
2. .If
3. .Al

1st verse

Jesus shed His precious blood and won the victory! He

1st verse

led captivity captive so that I would be free. In the

D.S.

Words and music: Copyright © Annette Willis 2010

In the power of His might... page 2

2nd verse
sa-tan tries to buff-et me, I ne-ver will des-pair; for by God's Word I am up-held, His truth is al-ways there. In the

3rd verse
though some batt-les I may face and hard times I may see, I know that He's pre-pared a place, pre-pared a place for me. And at the end of time I'll go to be with Christ the Lord; where He shall reign for-ev-er-more. I'll wor-ship and a-dore. In the

D.S. al Fine

Words and music: Copyright © Annette Willis 2010

6. Chosen by God

Annette Willis

♩ = 130 Con Moto

Cho-sen by God, I am cho-sen to be His for-ever, I am surr-end-ered to Him; for I am His child. I am a-dopt-ed as His child, He is my Fath-er for-ev-er, and His great love for me is... more than I can com-pre-hend, much

Words and music: Copyright © Annette Willis

more than I de-serve, that the Fath - er gave His
gift of love for me; for Je - sus died up -
on the cross and by His pre - cious blood, I'm acc -
ept - ed with - in God's fam - i - ly.
3
3
3

7. Holy God, yes You are a holy God
Annette Willis

♩ = 120

Holy God, yes You are a holy God; and how can I come before Your throne today? It's only by the precious blood of Jesus Christ; so cleanse my heart from ev'ry sin I pray.

Loving God, yes You are a loving God; and how can I show my love for You today? I know that You desire from me a lowly heart, that simply trusts and wants to go Your way.

CHORUS
And now I'm free to worship You in spirit and in

Words and Music: Copyright © Annette Willis 2010

truth, my love for You grows deep-er ev-'ry day.
When I think of all You've done, and the vic - tor - ies You've won,
and the love for me You've shown,
I want to bless You Lord, and lift Your Name on high,
I want to wor - ship Ho - ly God.
I want to love You, lov - ing God.

8. Blessèd be the Name of the Lord God Almighty

Annette Willis

Blessèd be the Name of the Lord God Almighty. Blessèd be the Name of Him who reigns on high. Blessèd be the Name, exalted in the heav'n-lies. Blessèd be the Name of Jesus Christ. For He is high and lifted up, His Name above all

Words and music: Copyright © Annette Willis 2010

Blessèd be the Name of the Lord God almighty... page 2

other names; and at His Name all knees shall bow,

when He comes a-gain. And Lord we hon-

-our You to-day and all that is with-in me cries:

"You are the Lord of all and worth-y of all

praise"

Words and music: Copyright © Annette Willis 2010

9. I can achieve all things that You've called me to do

Annette Willis

I can achieve all things that You've called me to do, my Father; for I can do all things through Christ who strengthens me. And I'm living under the covering of the pow'rful blood of Jesus, by which I'm cleansed, so I can truly be...

Words and music: Copyright © Annette Willis 2010

I can achieve all things that You've called me to do... page 2

a vess-el that's read-y for use by the Mast-er; I'm will-ing His call to o-bey. And the Ho-ly Spir-it lives with-in and em-pow-ers me for serv-ice; and He leads me and di-rects me all the way.

Words and music: Copyright © Annette Willis 2010

10. Jesus intercedes for me

Annette Willis

♩ = 88

Jesus is exalted in the highest; and His Name, above all other names. Yet He knows each trial we face, He's felt our pain and known our grief because as man on-to the earth He came. He ministered in love and pow'r, He healed the sick and lame, He set men free from all that bound. But

Words and music: Copyright © Annette Willis 2010

Jesus intercedes for me... page 2

now He is in Heav'n a-gain, His heart still full of love, the min-i-stry of Je-sus still a-bounds. Je-sus in-ter-cedes for me, when I just call u-pon His Name; why should I fear or be dis-mayed when He's pray-ing for me? Ev'ry night and ev'-ry day I bring my needs be-fore the Fath-er; and by His blood, God hears and an-swers ev'ry plea.

Words and music: Copyright © Annette Willis 2010

11. The place called Calvary

Annette Willis

Terr-i-ble place called Cal-va-ry where Je-sus, God's Son died for me.
Won-der-ful place called Cal-va-ry where Je-sus, God's Son died for me.

What dread-ful sights were seen that day be-cause the price of sin He'd pay. The crown of
What awe-some love was shown that day when Je-sus chose the Fath-er's way. "Fath-er for

Words and Music: Copyright © Annette Willis 2010

The place called Calvary... page 2

thorns, the cross, the nail; these He endured be-cause we'd
give them", Je-sus cried from on that cross be-fore He

failed. His pre-cious blood was shed for
died. Such love and mer - cy flowed for

me at that terr-i-ble place called Cal-va-ry.
me at that won-der-ful place called Cal-va-

ry. And I thank You to-day for Cal-va-ry!

Words and Music: Copyright © Annette Willis 2010

12. Love that gave itself for me

Annette Willis

Geth-sem-an-e, oh Geth-sem-an-e, where Je-sus was be-trayed. Son of God went un-to that place and to His Fath-er prayed, "If it's poss-i-ble, take this cup from me, yet not My will but

Cal-var-y, dread-ful Cal-var-y, the place where Je-sus died. Son of God nailed up-on a cross, un-just-ly cru-ci-fied. Yet ob-ed-ient-ly He took this path; it's hard to take it

Words and music: Copyright © Annette Willis 2010

Love that gave itself for me... page 2

Yours." He was re-solved to do God's will and
in, why He should choose a pain-ful death to

to de-fend His cause. Oh love that gave it-self for me, great
take a-way my sin.

love shown at Geth-sem-an-e; - and Lord, I give my love to
love was shown at Cal-var-y; and Lord, I give my life to

You, pre-cious Sa-viour, faith-ful and true.
You, pre-cious Sa-viour, faith-ful and true.

Words and music: Copyright © Annette Willis 2010

13. Walk tall my child

Annette Willis

♩ = 132

CHORUS

Walk tall my child; for I have broken the chains that once bound you. Walk tall my child; for my Spirit lives within you.

Last time to Coda

1st verse

The Father looked upon this earth and saw men bound by sin; but He had planned a way to reconcile mankind to Him. Walk you.

2nd verse

So God sent Jesus to the earth, His

Words and music: Copyright © Annette Willis 2010

Walk tall my child... page 2

2nd verse: life He freely gave. He shed His blood for each of us, our eternal souls to save. Walk you. The

3rd & 4th verse:
Son gave up His life for us to bring us liberty; and when He rose up from the dead, He won the victory!
So if you're bound by anything, just know this truth and say, "By His anointing and His blood, I can walk free today!" Walk you.

After 4th verse, D.S. al Coda

Words and music: Copyright © Annette Willis 2010

14. When I look at Your creation

Annette Willis

When I look at Your creation and I see the beauty there, I worship You, just worship You. When I recognise Your handiwork around me, ev'ry where, I worship You with all of my heart; for I'm Your creation too. I'm fearfully made, and wonderfully made by You. Yet in love You chose me to be Your child; and I love You Lord, with all of my heart.

Words and music: Copyright © Annette Willis 2010

15. In these last and final days before our Lord returns

Annette Willis

In these last and fi-nal days be-fore our Lord re-turns, we must pre-pare our hearts as His own bride; for the bride-groom is re-turn-ing to make His glor-y known, and with His rap-tured church He will a-bide. He's com-ing in splen-dour, He's com-ing in glor-y; and

Words and music: Copyright © Annette Willis 2010

In these last and final days... page 2

ev-'ry eye shall see Him, ev-'ry knee will bow, and all will re-cog-nise Him as the King of glor-y now. O Chri-stian re-joice! Our re-demp-tion has come. He is tak-ing us home. The fi-nal batt-le is won. There's no cry-ing there, there's no sick-ness, no pain. What a fu-ture we have... those who call on His Name.

Words and music: Copyright © Annette Willis 2010

16. When we look around us

Annette Willis

♩ = 88

When we look a-round us, see the state the world is in, we wonder why these things oc-cur... the e-vil and the sin; but then we read with-in God's Word and all be-comes quite clear, that in the Last Days we now live and Je-sus will soon ap-pear. And you don't know what will happ-en when you step out-side your door; for times, they will be per-i-lous and dan-ger is in store. So

Words and music: Copyright © Annette Willis 2010

When we look around us... page 2

seek the Saviour while you may and turn your heart from sin; for
He will lift His church away so we can be with Him.

There is a decision which all of us must make: eternal life, or eternal death... which pathway will you take? The right way is a narrow way, the wrong way, it is broad; the best way is to make the choice to follow Christ the Lord. And you

Fine

D.S. al Fine

Words and music: Copyright © Annette Willis 2010

17. When I look at my life

Annette Willis

When I look at my life, I see the mistakes I've made on the way; and sins of the past come back into my mind. But when I've repented, been cleansed by the blood, and sought forgiveness from God; I know that wonderful freedom can be mine.

Words and music: Copyright © Annette Willis 2010

When I look at my life.. page 2

Now there's no con-dem-na-tion for me, since Je-sus, God's Son set me free! Since I've re-ceived sal-va-tion, I've been set free from sin; not un-der con-dem-na-tion, but have perfect peace with-in. And Je-sus my re-deem-er

Words and music: Copyright © Annette Willis 2010

When I look at my life... page 3

would say now unto me... "Go in peace and sin no more; who the Son sets free is free!"

Slower
Thank You for Your blood, thank You for Your mercy, and Your grace, and this great sal-va-tion.

Slower
I thank You Lord!

Words and music: Copyright © Annette Willis 2010

18. Speak the Name of Jesus

Annette Willis

Speak the Name of Jesus, pray the Name of Jesus, declare the Name of Jesus; for He is the King. And His Name is mighty, and above all others. He is worthy of all praise, He's been exalted to the highest place. The precious Name of Jesus thrills my heart.

Words and music: Copyright © Annette Willis 2010

Speak the Name of Jesus... page 2

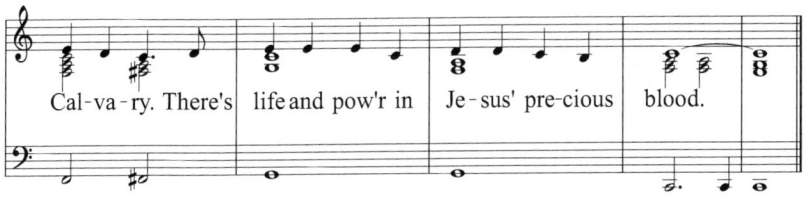

Plead the blood of Jesus, precious blood of Jesus, proclaim the blood of Jesus o-ver all your life; for His blood is cleans-ing and it is re-deem-ing. Our Lord shed His blood for me when He was cru-ci-fied at Cal-va-ry. There's life and pow'r in Jesus' pre-cious blood.

Words and music: Copyright © Annette Willis 2010

19. We are citizens of Heaven

Annette Willis

♩ = 100

We are ci-ti-zens of Heav-en and our Lord is com-ing soon. He will lift us up from all the earth and take our fear and gloom. It will be such joy to see Him, but re-mem-ber this my friend, be-fore the Lord re-turns, there's work to do; for He gave the great comm-iss-ion, which still we must o-bey, and the

Words and music: Copyright © Annette Willis 2010

We are citizens of heaven... page 2

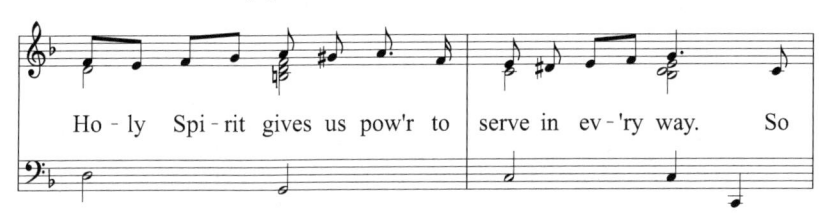

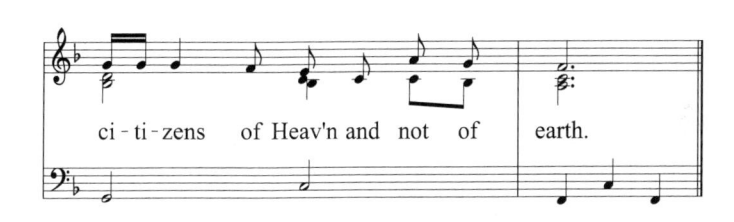

Ho - ly Spi - rit gives us pow'r to serve in ev - 'ry way. So choose to do His per-fect will and know this truth to-day... we are ci - ti - zens of Heav'n and not of earth.

Words and music: Copyright © Annette Willis 2010

20. This is a day of celebration

Annette Willis

This is a day of ce-le-bra-tion. This is a day to wor-ship God. This is a day of ju-bi-la-tion; and this is a day to praise the lord! I won't worr-y a-bout the past; from con-dem-na-tion Christ set me free! I have been gi-ven a brand new life; I live in Christ and Christ in

Words and music: Copyright © Annette Willis 2010

This is a day of celebration... page 2

me. I won't worry about the future, for it has enough cares of its own. I will centre my thoughts on Jesus, my peace is found in Him alone. All the time I know God is with me, and I freely can worship Him; I'm free to enter His glorious presence; free from care and free from sin.

Words and music: Copyright © Annette Willis 2010

21. God is mighty, strong to save

Annette Willis

God mighty, strong to save; He's my rock, I trust in Him.
When to Him, my life I gave, He rescued me from the pow'r of sin. We wrestle not with flesh and blood, but pow'rs and principalities; but God is mightier than the foe, and I know that He cares for me...

Words and music: Copyright © Annette Willis 2010

22. Reminders at Christmas time

Annette Willis

♩ = 92

Pre-sents giv-en to each oth-er, re-mind-ing us at Christ-mas time, that
Ca-rol sing-ing in the church-es, re-mind-ing us at Christ-mas time, of

God, our lov-ing heav'n-ly Fath-er, gave a gift so rare and fine; He
an-gels sing-ing songs of prais-es, tell-ing of the won-drous sign, That

Words and music: Copyright © Annette Willis 2010

Reminders at Christmas time... page 2

gave His one and on-ly Son, a gift of love for me. Re-
Je-sus came to earth from Heav-en, not as might-y King, but

ceive this gift with thank-ful heart and then the truth you'll see, that
as a help-less, hum-ble babe, His prais-es we should sing; for

Christ, the Sa-viour of the world, was babe and yet di-vine. Let's
Je-sus is now Lord of all, re-ceive Him while You may, give

ce-le-brate this Christ-mas time.
thanks to Him on Christ-mas day.

Words and music: Copyright © Annette Willis 2010

Reminders at Christmas time... page 3

Candles in the darkness burning, reminding us at Christmas time, that Jesus Christ, the light from Heaven came on this dark earth to shine. So let His light shine in your heart, let darkness fade away; His

Words and music: Copyright © Annette Willis 2010

Reminders at Christmas time... page 4

light will bring a bright new hope, He'll turn your night today. Let others see His light in you, proclaim Him as your King and make Him Lord of ev-'ry thing. This Christmas, worship Christ the King!

Rallentando

Words and music: Copyright © Annette Willis 2010

23. A promise through the ages

Annette Willis

A promise through the ages had been giv'n by God to man, that to our world a Saviour would come. For man had drifted far from God when sin had entered in; then

Words and music: Copyright © Annette Willis 2010

A promise through the ages... page 2

Je - sus came, the pre - cious prom - ised One.

For He came... the prom-ised Mess - i -

- ah. And He came... the hope of all the earth. Yet He came...

leav-ing all of His glor - y; in a sta-ble was His

Words and music: Copyright © Annette Willis 2010

A promise through the ages... page 3

hum-ble birth. For He left all the glor-y of Heav-en, be-cause God had a heart of love for man. And at Chist-mas time let's re-mem-ber that Je-sus came as ful-fil-ment of God's plan... re-deem-ing

Words and music: Copyright © Annette Willis 2010

A promise through the ages... page 4

plan. For He came... the prom-ised Mess-i - - ah. And one day He'll come to earth a - gain; not as babe in a poor hum-ble sta- ble, but as great might-y King come to reign. When Je-sus comes in-to your heart He'll

Words and music: Copyright © Annette Willis 2010

A promise through the ages... page 5

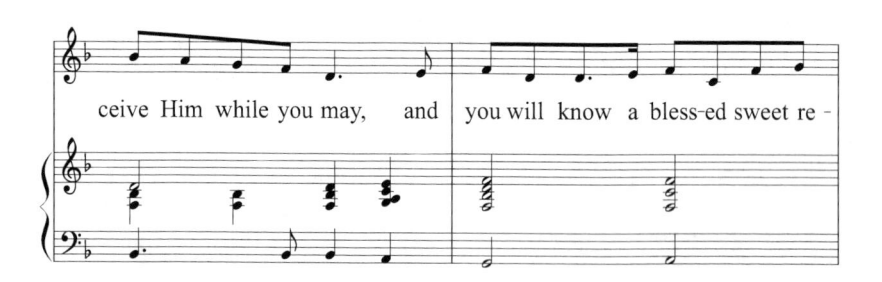

take your sin a-way, He'll give you joy that lasts and per-fect peace. So just be-lieve His love for you, re-ceive Him while you may, and you will know a bless-ed sweet re-lease. For He came... the prom-ised Mess-i

Words and music: Copyright © Annette Willis 2010

A promise through the ages... page 6

ah. Prince of peace, and Jesus was His Name. So at Christ - mas give Him your prais - es, and rejoice in your heart that He came... that Jesus came... I'm so glad He came.

Rallentando

Words and music: Copyright © Annette Willis 2010

24. We're in the presence of the King

Annette Willis

We're in the presence of the King.
Lift up your voice and praises sing.
This place is holy, for He's here.
Come bow in reverence and fear;
for King Jesus, You are great beyond compare,
like a jewel that is precious, yet so rare.
Lord, we honour You and give the glory due;
Son of God, eternal King.

Words and music: Copyright © Annette Willis 2010

25. I hear the sound of heavy rain

Annette Willis

♩ = 100

I hear the sound of heav-y rain, it's coming! It's coming! Look for the signs, have faith a-gain, I know it's com-ing soon. The thir-sty land will be re-vived when the rain comes, the rain comes. Just see the cloud; the rain is on its way. We've prayed for the rain to come on our land; the rain of God's Spir-it to pour down. We've

Words and music: Copyright © Annette Willis 2010

I hear the sound of heavy rain... page 2

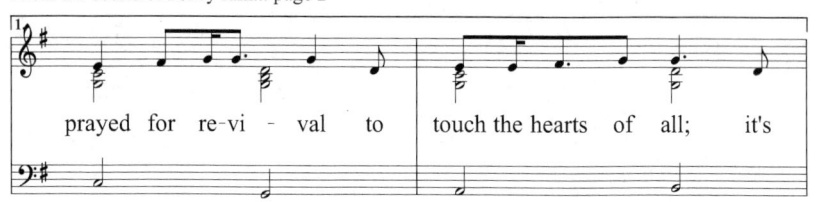

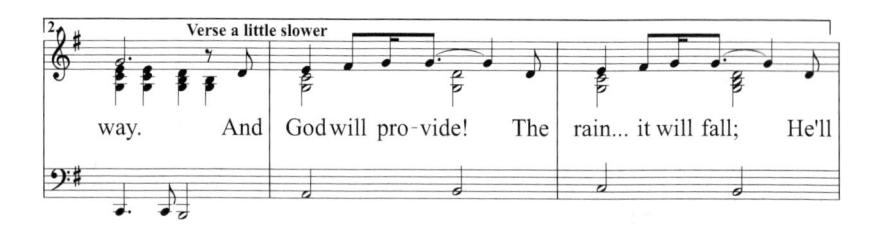

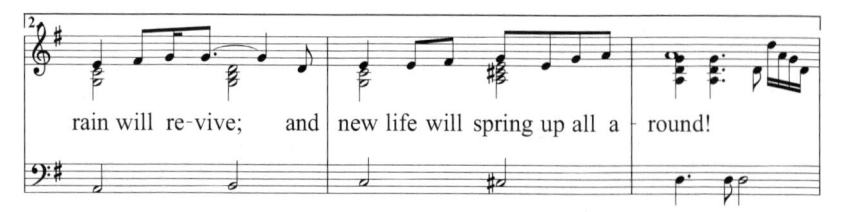

I hear the sound of heavy rain... page 3

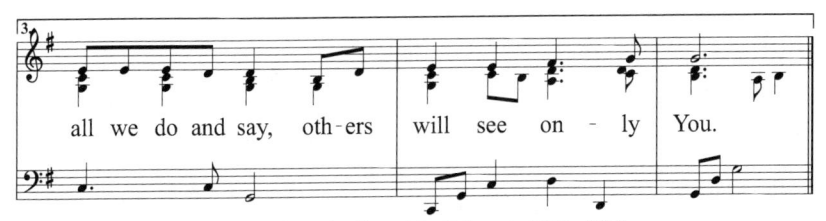

I way. Yes, God's latt-er rain has start-ed to fall, we know He is mov-ing in this place. He's touched us with His pow'r, He's touched us with His love, He's been right here with us by His grace.

Rallentando

Much slower, decrease tempo until end

We thank You Lord, make us vess-els now for You, that in all we do and say, oth-ers will see on-ly You.

Words and music: Copyright © Annette Willis 2010

26. Lord Jesus, I am so amazed

Annette Willis

Lord Jesus, I am so a-mazed that though You were a-ware of all the suff'ring You'd en-dure, the pain You'd have to bear; and know the hate in peop-le's eyes, the hate-ful words they'd cry, to know the pain You'd have to take... an awe - some sacri

Words and music: Copyright © Annette Willis 2010

Lord Jesus, I am so amazed... page 2

fice. You knew full well the Father's plan, yet chose not to decline; and this great act of love from You has touched my heart and mind. Lord, I'm so glad You chose to take this way of pain for me; that You took all my sin and shame when nailed upon that tree. For You are now my righteousness, salvation and my joy, my

Words and music: Copyright © Annette Willis 2010

Lord Jesus, I am so amazed... page 3

peace and my de-liv-er-ance from all that could de-stroy; and death was not the end for You, to life You rose a-gain. Your vic-t'ry is my vic-t'ry too, if in You I re-main.

Slower ♩ = 63

My off-er-ing of gra-ti-tude in words, app-ears so small, so Lord, I give my heart to You, my

Rallentando to end

love, my life, my all.

Words and music: Copyright © Annette Willis 2010